.

Newton's Laws

The C.M. Newton Story

Newton's Laws

The C.M. Newton Story as told to Billy Reed

Host Communications, Inc.
Lexington, Kentucky

"Newton's Laws" is published by Host Communications, Inc.,
904 North Broadway, Lexington, Kentucky 40505.
W. James Host, Publisher; Eric Barnhart, President;
Mark Coyle, Senior Vice President/Publishing

Project Manager: Kim Ramsay
Promotions and distribution by Caroline Taylor, Tim Francis
Edited by David Kaplan
Design by Dan Shute

Photography provided by: USA Basketball, David Coyle, Breck Smither,
Doug Brachey, NBA Photos, Lexington Herald-Leader, Transylvania University
Special Collections. Some photos provided by the University of Kentucky,
University of Alabama and Vanderbilt University media relations offices.
Some photos from C.M. Newton's personal collection.

ISBN: 1-57640-055-7

The faculty and staff of UK HealthCare are proud to help sponsor this publication honoring Coach C.M. Newton. Over the years, Coach Newton has inspired greatness in all of us with his commitment to providing challenges to young athletes and instilling in each a sense of integrity and discipline required to succeed not only in college athletics, but also in life.

At UK HealthCare, we follow Coach Newton's lead by inspiring greatness in the field of medicine. We strive to achieve Top 20 academic medical center status through innovative thinking and research, compassion and a true commitment to the communities we serve throughout Kentucky. We've found no better role model to help us achieve great things than in him. And for that, we are all grateful and feel privileged to call him a valued member of the UK family.

Acknowledgements

I found this assignment to be the most difficult part of this project. Three basic questions surfaced: How do I adequately express appreciation to all of those who have been an important part of my life? Do I dare name some people knowing that time, space and memory will not permit me to name all who have been significant in my life? In acknowledging a lifetime in athletics, do I identify events, games, places, job opportunities, etc. or people?

Let me begin with a special thank you to Jim Host — long-time friend, confidant, consultant and adviser. It was Jim's insistence that "there's a book in you" and for his willingness to take the risk in publishing it, I am grateful. And thanks to "one of my boys," Billy Reed — former student and long-time friend, Hall of Fame sports journalist and strong advocate for "doing it right" in athletics — for his expertise in researching, organizing and writing this book.

On to the questions — in reverse order. It is my strong belief that acknowledgement and appreciation must be given to people. Regardless of one's vocation or profession, we are all in the "people business." Ultimately, our success or failure will depend upon our people skills and our ability to nurture relationships. I was privileged to have the playing field, the gymnasium, the university setting and the home in which to interact with people and to form relationships. As I look back, people and relationships — not events, games, places, job opportunities, etc. — were the most important and significant part of my life.

I have chosen not to name individuals out of concern for time and space and due to my fear of omitting someone significant to me. Instead, I will list categories of people and relationships that were meaningful to me. Hopefully all who read this book will recognize the important role you played in the following categories:

1. My family — with much love to all members of my immediate and extended family.

2. My former players — you are the "heart" of an athletics program. You taught me much more than I taught you!

3. My teammates — sharing and caring was our gift to each other.

4. My coaches and mentors — you molded and shaped me.

5. My coaching friends and opposing coaches — we learned from each other.

6. The presidents and administrators I worked for — I borrowed from each of you.

7. My co-workers — sincere appreciation for the loyalty, dedication and expertise given by all assistant coaches, support staff, secretaries, managers and trainers.

8. My special friends and supporters — you are each unique and special in your own way.

9. The NCAA basketball staff and committee members — thank you for your guardianship of the NCAA Tournament, your integrity and your fairness.

10. The USA Basketball and FIBA staffs and offices — thanks for making a great American game a great game for the entire world.

11. The members of the media — you have an important job, strive to do it well.

12. The game officials — you are critical to the success and integrity of the game.

13. The fans and supporters of intercollegiate athletics — pull hard for your team, have fun and keep athletics in its proper perspective.

Finally, the key question: How do I adequately express appreciation to all of those people who have been an important part of my life? Someone once said, "actions speak louder than words." I hope, by my actions, that each of you know of my sincere appreciation for what you have meant to me. Finally, I have always believed that if one is reduced to using words instead of actions to express appreciation, it is best to be simple and direct.

Putting that belief into action, *Thank You!!!*

C.M. Newton
January 10, 2000

To my family:

Mom, Dad, Jean, Richard and Bill — my roots

Mr. & Mrs. Davis and Shirley — Evelyn's Mom & Dad and sister

*Deborah, Tracy and Martin — three special, different
and unique children, now adults*

Cindy and Phil — Martin and Tracy's spouses

*Katie, Madison, Zach, Joshua and Sheridan —
my five "favorite" (and only) grandchildren*

*A special dedication to Evelyn, who has shared most of
my 69 years either as my friend, lover, wife, mother of our
children, grandmother, coaching associate, counselor or
confidant. Evelyn is truly "hard to guard" yet she is
the most genuinely caring person I've ever known.*

*I have been blessed to have a family that was
supportive of me, that shared in the good and
the bad times and whose love was always present.
I love, admire and respect each of you very much.*

Foreword
by Cawood Ledford

"Mama called." That was the simple yet concise way that Paul "Bear" Bryant, the great football coach, explained his decision to leave his powerful football program at Texas A&M and return to Alabama, his alma mater, to rebuild the fallen fortunes of the Crimson Tide.

C.M. Newton, a great admirer of Coach Bryant, could have used the same two words when C.M.'s alma mater, the University of Kentucky, sent out the S.O.S in 1989. Had it not been "Mama" who called, I doubt C.M. would have accepted the tremendous challenge he saw at his old school. He was an established basketball coach at an established program, Vanderbilt, where he also served as associate athletics director.

No one could remember when Kentucky's basketball program had been in such dire straits. The NCAA had been investigating UK's recruiting practices for more than a year and handed out severe sanctions at the end of the 1988-89 season. No television appearances for one year. No post-season play for two years. Players transferred.

On April 1, 1989, C.M. left his secure, fulfilling position at Vandy to take over the athletics director's role at UK and the awful mess that awaited at his old school.

"Mama" had called.

His first order of business was to smooth the troubled waters of the basketball program by hiring Rick Pitino as the coach. By his third season, the Wildcats won the SEC Tournament and advanced to the Elite Eight of the NCAA Tournament before losing to No. 1-ranked Duke in overtime.

Now, looking back on 11 years as the top gun in the UK athletics department, C.M. can point to two NCAA championships (1996 and 1998) and the restoration of UK among the top echelon of college basketball.

With the basketball program back in full swing, C.M. turned to UK's struggling football program. Three years ago, he brought Hal Mumme on campus to coach the Wildcats. Hal brought an exciting, wide-open style of play that has excited fans all across the Commonwealth. Mumme's last two teams have gone to postseason bowls. Under Newton's watch, Nutter Field House was built and Commonwealth Stadium was expanded.

I knew that C.M. had been a member of Coach Adolph Rupp's NCAA championship team in 1951, but I first met him during his coaching stint at Transylvania where he built that program into one of the best in the small college division. I got to know him better while broadcasting Kentucky basketball during C.M.'s two coaching stops in the SEC, first at Alabama, where Bryant brought him in to rebuild, then later at Vanderbilt. C.M.'s coaching record is tremendously impressive but it soars when you consider that at each stop he took a down-and-out program and built it into a winner.

C.M. Newton has been a winner his entire life and has won while playing by all the rules. He has never been touched by even so much as a hint of scandal. He has solidified the Kentucky program and he has done so within the rules.

C.M. Newton is one of the most caring and ethical people whom it has been my pleasure to know. He is highly regarded wherever college or amateur sports are played. Coach Bryant once said "C.M. Newton is a winner, and that's important, but more than anything else, he wins or loses with class, and that's more important."

C.M. held Bryant in high regard and he often says that the highest compliment Bryant could give a person was to say that a person had class. Bryant said, "I can't describe class, but I know it when I see it." Well, I do too. C.M. Newton has class with a capital "C."

Cawood Ledford
January 4, 2000

Introduction
by Billy Reed

I didn't play basketball for C.M. Newton when I was a student at Transylvania University from 1962-66, but I've always thought of myself as one of his "boys." He was a mentor to me at a time when I really needed one. So despite the fact that I've worked for a lot of talented and inspirational editors in my 41-year sportswriting career, I'll always give Coach Newton enormous credit for changing my life and shaping my values.

In the spring of 1962, after a frustrating freshman year at the University of Kentucky, I was about as confused and unhappy as an 18-year-old kid could be. I wanted to go to college, like most of my friends from Henry Clay High School, but I didn't have the money. My parents had just gone through an ugly divorce. I was already working full-time at *The Lexington Leader* to support myself and do what I could to help my mother and two sisters.

I figured there was no way I could ever get my college degree, so I decided to quit school and concentrate on my job. At the time, the newspaper's sports editor was making something like $125 a week, which seemed like big money. Maybe, I thought, I would someday reach that level.

One of my beats for *The Leader* was Transylvania sports. So one day, after an interview, I spilled my guts to Coach Newton, who always had seemed to be a good listener. When I was done, he urged me to stay in school. "Come to Transylvania," he told me, "and I'll try to help you get some money. But don't quit. You might not believe it now, but that degree will be awfully important to you someday."

True to his word, he helped me get some financial aid by giving me a part-time job as his student sports information director. I vaguely remember pounding out a few news releases in a stuffy office somewhere in McAlister Auditorium. I didn't do a very good job, I'm afraid, but Coach Newton never complained. He just chastised me every now and then for spending too much time at the newspaper (or with my fraternity brothers) and not enough in the Transylvania library.

In those days, the newspaper office was on Short Street, just behind the courthouse and only a couple of blocks from the Transylvania campus. So a typical day for me would go like this: Work from 7 a.m. to 10 a.m. Walk to Transylvania and take classes from 10 a.m. to 2 p.m. Go back to the office and work a couple more hours getting ready for the next day's paper. My evenings would be spent studying, dating or covering a high school game.

It was during this time that I met another gentleman who had a profound effect on my values. His name was S.T. Roach and he was the head basketball coach at Dunbar, one of the two all-black high schools in Lexington. Without ever preaching, Coach Roach taught me much about dignity and decency. Although there were times when I was the only white person at a Dunbar game, I was never mistreated. Coach Roach saw to that. Because of him, I came to understand the terrible unfairness and injustice inherent in a segregated society. To myself, I vowed to do anything I could, as a journalist, to promote the ideals of integration and equal rights.

Years later, when Coach Newton nominated Tubby Smith to be the first African-American head coach of the men's basketball team at UK, the nomination was seconded by Coach Roach, who had long been a member of the university's athletics board. At that moment, a lot of powerful memories came together for me. I'm confident that I was as proud and happy as anybody in the room.

But I digress.

Besides being the basketball coach at Transylvania, Coach Newton also taught a few courses every quarter by virtue of his role as head of the physical education department. I took one of them, "Introduction to Basketball" or something like that. I know it sounds like a piece of cake, but don't laugh. For an aspiring sportswriter, it was as valuable as any English or history course.

From Coach Newton, I learned the principles of various offenses and defenses, the advantages and liabilities of each and how to decide game strategy based on your material and that of your opponent. But as much as he taught me about basketball, he taught me even more about values.

He preached that winning was important only if it was done within the context of honesty and integrity, that lying and cheating were unacceptable and that college athletes were students first and foremost. I never forgot that. If anybody were to review my editorial positions over more than four decades, I think he or she would find that I've consistently supported coaches who operated within the rules and criticized those who didn't. That comes directly from Coach Newton.

Because of Coach Newton, I got a B.A. in English from Transylvania in 1966. And that opened the door for opportunities that otherwise would never have existed.

When Coach Newton left Transylvania for Alabama in 1968, I was apprehensive. Not because I doubted his ability to coach against the best, but because I was afraid he would get eaten alive by the cheaters in the recruiting process. I feared he was too decent a man to turn around a program that had been one of the Southeastern Conference's worst. Well, silly me. He built Alabama into a championship program by becoming the first league coach to engage in the wholesale recruitment of black players.

In the fall of 1999, I accompanied Coach Newton and his family to Tuscaloosa for a reunion of Alabama players. At the banquet, one player after another, black and white, talked about the difference he had made in their lives. As I listened to the likes of Wendell Hudson, Robert Scott and Reggie King, I felt extraordinarily proud. He never won a national championship during his coaching days, but I'll argue that he won an even larger victory.

When Coach Newton retired from coaching in 1989 to return to UK as Athletics Director, I wrote this for the *Herald-Leader*: "As for me, I feel better about the future of UK athletics than I have in years. Others have heard about C.M. Newton's character, but I know, from personal experience, what kind of man he is." Well, to put it mildly, he more than justified my confidence in him.

When I was selected to the U.S. Basketball Writers Hall of Fame, the committee told me to pick somebody to introduce me. The first name that came to mind was C.M. Newton. He agreed, and the ceremony took place on Monday, April 1, 1996, at the Marriott in downtown New York. His remarks were typically gracious and overly flattering. I'll always be grateful that he took the time to do that for me on the day the Wildcats defeated Syracuse to win the university its first NCAA championship since 1978.

From the time I met him until today, Coach Newton has never really changed. The more success he has enjoyed, and the more money he has made, the more determined he seems to remain rooted in the values that have guided him throughout his life. Whenever I would suggest that he should do a book, he would laugh and say something like, "Why would anybody want to read about me?" So I was thrilled when he called in August 1999, to say that he had changed his mind and to ask if I would be interested in helping him write this book.

He didn't have to pick me because he has other friends who are accomplished journalists. But I suppose it was just another example of him being loyal to one of his "boys." At least, that's the way I will always prefer to look at it. We had a wonderful time working together, jogging each other's memory and swapping stories about mutual friends. There was a lot of laughter. I just hope our finished product is an interesting and accurate reflection of this special person's remarkable life.

Billy Reed
December 23, 1999

Chapter 1
Sunshine and Storms

T o this day, I can't imagine a better place to grow up than Fort Lauderdale, Fla., in the 1930s and '40s. There was the sun and the beaches, which were great for a kid who loved all kinds of sports. And it wasn't a big city in those days, maybe 20,000 or so year-round residents. So my growing-up memories are mostly happy ones, although in my early childhood there was a problem with my dad that has lingered with me throughout my adult life. My dad was an alcoholic, a binge drinker, who achieved sobriety when I was about 10 years old.

As I know now, alcoholism is a family disease that affects every member of the family. Yet in spite of the family problems, I was blessed with a mother and father who genuinely loved and cared for each other and their children. Additionally, I was lucky to have some male role models in the form of a coach, a minister and a family friend, each of whom mentored me during my formative years. To aspiring coaches, I can't emphasize enough the importance not only of teaching youngsters to play games, but to also be role models and mentors in their personal lives.

I was born in Rockwood, Tenn., on Feb. 2, 1930, and I was called C.M., for Charles Martin, almost from the cradle. We had other Charleses and Martins in the family, so I was C.M. When I was around nine months old, my mom and dad moved our family — I had an older brother, Richard, and a sister, Jean — to Fort Lauderdale. That was right in the middle of The Great Depression, and Dad had family there who could give us some help and support.

My dad, Richard Yates Newton, only had a sixth-grade education, but I always felt he was one of the smartest men I ever knew. He quit school to work for the railroad, and later got involved in the hardware business. I remember him selling Maytag washers. He and my mom, Adelia Martin Newton, had grown up together in Roane County in east Tennessee and had married at a fairly young age. He was a good father and a good husband, but his addiction to alcohol was a problem that impacted the entire family. Jean, who was 12 years older than I, was affected the most by Dad's drinking. Richard and I were considerably younger when he achieved sobriety.

We lived in town, a block away from Fort Lauderdale High School, a campus that housed the elementary, junior high and senior high. Therefore, I had the luxury of going from grades 1 through 12 in the same school. I could walk to school and spend most of my free time in the gym or on an athletic field. Mom and Dad ran a rooming and boarding house. Mom did the cooking and baking, and we lived off the roomers and boarders. Although the tourist season was the busiest time, it was a year-round operation. She would start cooking early in the morning, then serve lunch and dinner, family-style, with the boarders getting the first call. Dad handled the business part of it, but Mom was the catalyst who kept the business together. I will always remember how hard Mom worked.

When I was about 10, Dad's drinking had gotten to be such a problem that Mom threatened to move us back to Tennessee with her family. Jean had already married, so there was only Richard and myself at home. It was at this point that Mom and Dr. Edward P. Downey, a Presbyterian minister, convinced Dad that he needed help. Dr. Downey was the first person I can remember who called Dad's drinking an illness, something that he could not help doing or solve by himself. I had always assumed that his drinking was due to a weakness in character or a lack of willpower.

At any rate, Dad made the first step to recovery by going to Miami and entering a sanatorium under a physician's care. Achieving sobriety was life-changing for Dad and the entire family. As a result of this storm in my early life, I have spent most of my adult life trying to learn more about alcoholism and how to deal with it in my family, with my players and with others. Dr. and Mrs. Downey played a vital role in the lives of our family and I always will be grateful for the genuine Christian love and care they gave to each of us.

When Dad got sober, everything really changed for us. It was around the time that America became involved in World War II, but Dad wasn't able to serve in the military because of physical problems. Farming was a way to help the war effort, so Dad bought property west of town and we moved to the country to raise hogs and do some truck farming for produce. We were middle class — not poor, but not with a lot of extras, either. Dad, Richard, Mr. Stanky (a hired hand) and I would go to the nearby Naval Air Station to get swill for hogs.

I also sold newspapers at the Naval Air Station and this gave me a chance to observe athletics at a highly competitive level. I had my horse, Rocket, and fancied myself as a real cowboy. We had a four-acre, spring-fed, fresh-water lake that Dad stocked with bass and bream. It also became the home of Old Joe, a very large alligator. I had a lot of time to myself. I'd shoot baskets at an outdoor goal, and fish and hunt by myself. This was a valuable experience for me. I learned to be alone without being lonely.

During this time, Richard and Jean developed a special bond and a very close relationship. Jean had a strong influence on Richard, and I'm sure this was one of the reasons that he became interested in West Point and a potential military career. Dad didn't have the political clout to get Richard an appointment at West Point, so Richard, at Jean's urging, prepared himself for the competitive entrance exam. As I watched Richard prepare for the exam, I had no doubt he would be successful. He was admitted to West Point, graduated in the class of 1950, was commissioned and had a successful 30-year career in the Air Force.

As is the case with almost everyone, I've had more than a few heroes in my life. But no one was, or is, a bigger hero to me than Richard. As I went through school, he was really a tough act to follow. While I was a decent student, he set the curve. Our aunt, Ruth Hendrick, was an English teacher in high school. One day during my senior year, she said, "Well, you're not anything like your brother," and predicted that I wouldn't even be an average student in college. That really motivated me. Years later, when I went to Alabama to get my doctorate, I reminded her of what she had told me.

When Richard left for West Point in 1946, my life changed again. From him I inherited my first car, a used 1939 green Buick, and I remember Dad saying, "You better not get caught speeding." Well, the first night, I was driving around with Dick Esterline and I got caught doing 35 in a 25-mile-an-hour zone. I panicked. If Dad found out, there went the car. Dick's father came down and paid the

$15 fine. When I got home, Mom and Dad both were asleep. But I woke up Mom and said, "I need to talk to you." I told her what happened and she agreed to keep it from Dad.

Well, he was a voracious reader. He read the *Fort Lauderdale News* from cover to cover. So I got home the next day and took the paper before he could get it. He fussed and fumed for two or three days about the paper boy. But then he came home one day just furious. It seems he had been walking down the street and one of his friends said, "I see where C.M. made the paper again." At first he assumed it was because of a baseball game. But when he found out about the ticket, he came home and really got after Mom and me.

Because of the car, I had the freedom to play fast-pitch softball, semi-pro baseball and basketball in the summer. Mom was the one who convinced Dad that I could handle this newfound freedom. She was the family's spiritual leader. She had such a deep and abiding faith that she could find the good in almost any situation. If I needed something, she would find a way to get it done. I can still hear her saying, "Okay, this time, but don't tell your dad." It was also during this time that Jean and I developed a special sister-younger brother relationship.

Dad exposed me to baseball at an early age, taught me to hunt and fish and showed me how to be responsible financially. He was a trader and a good businessman. He eventually took that farm and sold it off in lots. He impressed two financial ideas on me that I have carried throughout my life. First, he told me to not invest in anything that eats while you sleep, which was the reason I never considered entering the horse business in Kentucky. The other was that if you borrow money, make sure you can pay it back quickly. As Dad said, "Interest works 24 hours a day and will always outwork you."

One of the most positive things that Mom and Dad gave each of us was the freedom to do things. Freedom to risk, freedom to succeed, freedom to fail. Maybe that's the best kind of parenting. I always had good supervision from my parents, but they'd let me go with Doyle McNeese, a good athlete who was my sister's age, to watch him play in semi-pro baseball and fast-pitch softball games. And they'd let me spend time with Clois Caldwell, the basketball coach and assistant football coach at Fort Lauderdale High.

At a time when Dad was still struggling with his sobriety, Coach Caldwell really took me under his wing and became an important mentor for me. Beginning when I was about 10 or so, he would encourage me to hang around practice and go on road trips with the team. He had great success as a basketball coach, but I don't remember him raising his voice or swearing. He was just an outstanding teacher/coach, and he took a real liking to me. We won state championships in basketball and baseball when I played for him. We just had a real special relationship, to the point that when he died years later, his wife asked me to be the speaker at his funeral service.

As a young athlete, I always played with older guys, and as a result, I experienced success earlier than most. I received a lot of positive reinforcement out of that early success. I started on the varsity basketball team as a ninth grader and became the starting quarterback in football as a sophomore. It was an era where youngsters weren't forced to specialize in a single sport, which is the situation most young people face today. We played the sport that was in season and spent our free time, out of season, on the sport you liked the most. Also, there were no organized leagues for youngsters of elementary school or junior high age. We got together, picked our teams and played games. No adult coaches, no officials, no uniforms. One of my biggest thrills was making the team in high school so I could finally have a uniform and play for a coach. When you contrast that to the pressures and excesses of today's youth programs, you can make a strong argument for the "good old days."

I loved basketball because you could play it by yourself, year-round, down on the outdoor courts at the beaches, where everyone hung out. I loved football because it's the ultimate team game and because of the excitement around the games. And I loved baseball because that was *the* professional sport in those days. Dad used to take me, on a regular basis, to watch the local Class D team, the Fort Lauderdale Tarpons. The Boston Braves trained in Fort Lauderdale during the spring, and I once got to be their batboy, giving me the chance to be around Billy Southworth, then the Braves' manager. Most young athletes in those days wanted to become big-league players, and I was no exception.

With the different odd jobs I had around town — I sold newspapers, pumped gas, things like that — I was around black kids. You didn't think anything about it. If my family did me any favor, it was to convince me that you treated people with respect if you expected to get respect in return. Sometimes we'd go to what was then called "colored town" and play pickup games with blacks on outdoor courts and fields. When I was very young, I remember hearing tales about the lynching of a black man west of Fort Lauderdale. But I heard a lot more criticism about Jews than blacks. It was not uncommon to have "restricted clientele" signs in the hotels, meaning Jews weren't allowed. I just could never understand that. Our biggest rival was Miami Beach High, which was predominantly Jewish. But when you played sports, you just never paid attention to color, race or religion.

Beginning with my sophomore year in high school, another important influence came into my life. Her name was Evelyn Davis. We originally met in the first grade. I remember playing football with her at night by the light coming out of the post office windows. But her family moved away, and then they moved back in my sophomore year in high school. I was just starting to get interested in girls, and we began dating. She was an outstanding athlete — a diver, tennis player and cheerleader. We became really good friends before we fell in love and started dating seriously during our senior year, even talking about getting married someday.

Evelyn would go with me to my summer basketball and baseball games, but more than that, she was supportive in ways that I wasn't even aware of at the time. Dad was doing great and Evelyn didn't know until much later in our marriage that he had ever had a problem with alcohol. When she found out, she was quite upset with me for not telling her. But family secrets are another spinoff from the disease of alcoholism. When we finished high school, Evelyn went to the University of Miami on a diving scholarship. We agreed that we would continue to "go steady," but would also date others and enjoy college life.

I knew I wanted to someday play professional baseball, but there weren't many schools that offered baseball scholarships back then. Coach Caldwell wanted me to look at Oklahoma A&M — he was a disciple of Hank Iba, the great basketball coach who had won NCAA titles in 1945 and '46 — along with Duke, Illinois and Tennessee. I wanted to go to Tennessee because of my family's roots, but they wouldn't recruit me as anything other than a football player.

And then there was Kentucky.

In those days there was no TV, so we got our live news from the radio and the Movietone News at the theater. And it seemed that all you heard regarding basketball — the NBA didn't amount to much in those days — was Kentucky and Coach Adolph Rupp. They had won the NIT, which then was bigger than the NCAA Tournament, in 1946. UK won the NCAA in 1948 with the team known as "The Fabulous Five." They had offered me a scholarship, and with Coach Caldwell urging me to go to Lexington to see the program for myself, I visited the UK campus in June 1948, while UK was playing host to the Olympic Trials.

The nucleus of the 1948 Olympic squad consisted of the five Kentucky starters (Alex Groza, Ralph Beard, Wah Wah Jones, Kenny Rollins and Cliff Barker), and the five starters from the Phillips 66ers, the national AAU champions. A huge crowd watched the Wildcats play the 66ers on a portable court that had been set up in the middle of Stoll Field, where the Wildcats played football. I couldn't have been in Lexington at a more exciting time, and I wanted to come to UK after that experience.

Coach Rupp was the reason I came to UK. Just meeting him and seeing what basketball meant to him — that was enough for me. I came to Kentucky to compete for playing time in a great program with great players, but I also had been assured that I could play baseball. My dream of playing professional baseball was still alive and well. In those days, UK was about the only Southeastern Conference school that emphasized basketball. For example, I was one of 10 scholarship freshmen at Kentucky at the same time Florida was giving only two basketball scholarships.

It was tough to leave Evelyn and my family, but I was excited about college. Coach Caldwell had suggested that after I graduated, if I didn't make it in professional baseball, he would become athletics director at Fort Lauderdale High and I would replace him as basketball coach. With that comforting thought tucked away, I headed off to Lexington to see if I could make it in the biggest and most glamorous program in college basketball.

Chapter 2
A Shetland Pony in a
Stud-Horse Parade

In 1948, Lexington was quite a town. A racy town, if you will, and I'm not just talking about the horse races at Keeneland. Under Coach Rupp in basketball and Paul "Bear" Bryant in football, UK was in the midst of a golden era of prosperity and success. Wildcat athletes were big men, not only on campus but around town, and there were a lot of boosters in the nightclubs and bars who liked to brag that they were close to the program. Gambling on sports, as illegal then as it is today, nevertheless was popular. A bookmaker named Ed Curd had a room above Mayfair Bar on East Main where there were teletype machines, all the better to get the scores for gamblers.

Coming in as a freshman in 1948, I was oblivious to all this. Here I was, more than 1,000 miles from home in a whole different world. I was excited, but apprehensive at the same time. That first winter, I saw my first snow. I had an English professor who asked us to write a theme about something that was new to us. On the first day it snowed,

I was sitting in English class. The professor said, "Mr. Newton, look out the window ... That is snow ... You may be excused." And I went out and experienced the snow.

Another big thing was that the veterans were back from World War II. The basketball team had guys like Cliff Barker, who had learned to be an excellent ball-handler while killing time in a prisoner-of-war camp, and Dale Barnstable, who also had been in the service. Some of Coach Bryant's football players also were veterans. So for those of us fresh out of high school, from the first day we stepped on campus, it was the greatest eye-opening experience you could have.

In those days, the NCAA's main focus was its championships and it implemented few recruiting restrictions. The conferences were the strength and there were unlimited scholarships in football. Coach Bryant literally brought 'em in by the truckload and tried 'em out. He coached by attrition. Every day, his players had to prove their manhood. As I got to know him later at Alabama, he told me he probably ran off more good players than he coached.

At that time, Coach Bryant didn't have the national reputation that Coach Rupp had. Coach Rupp had won the NIT in 1946 when it was *the* major tournament in college basketball. But he came to strongly support the NCAA Tournament because of his ties to the National Association of Basketball Coaches, which started a national tournament in

1939 and ran it until the NCAA took it over a year later. Coach Bryant was a very handsome young man who had almost a movie-star quality about him. He also had a certain atmosphere of aloofness which I later found out was really shyness. Coach Rupp also was very imposing, but in a different sort of way.

They were more alike than they were different. They both motivated with fear. Heck, I stayed scared of Coach Rupp the whole time I was in school. Both also were sticklers for detail. I used to watch the football practices, and I probably learned as much about coaching basketball from Coach Bryant as I did from anybody. He emphasized situation practices, saving timeouts until the end of games, things like that. Coach Rupp emphasized fundamentals, pressure defense, game preparation and paying attention to the little things. His practices were timed to the second and they were strictly business. He had a saying, "Don't speak unless you can improve the silence," and that's the way he ran our practices.

In 1948-49, I was on Harry Lancaster's first freshman team. He was Coach Rupp's top assistant and he had a great basketball mind. Over the years, Harry had several chances to go somewhere as a head coach, but he stayed with Coach Rupp until becoming UK's Athletics Director in 1968. We played before every varsity game at home and went on the road a few times. But the most awesome thing was practicing against the varsity because they were the best team in the country. They had four starters back from the "Fabulous Five" team of 1948 — Ralph Beard, Barker, Alex Groza and Wah Wah Jones — and they had a lot of other good players such as Barnstable, Jim Line and Walt Hirsch. Those guys were older and more mature than us, but we had good players such as Bill Spivey, Bobby Watson, Skippy Whitaker, Guy Strong and Shelby Linville. I got real homesick as a freshman. Evelyn was at Miami and I missed her. But Beard and Humzey Yessin, our team manager, were a great help to me.

I started a lot on the freshman team and had a chance to play some as a sophomore in 1949-50 because the varsity, which had won the NCAA title for the second straight year, lost four starters. The motivation was to play well enough in practice to travel with the varsity. Coach Rupp believed in playing only eight guys. He treated them like the good guys and the rest like ... well, he called the rest his 'turd squad.' As a player, you really tried hard to be one of the good guys. I felt I had a good year in freshman basketball, and I enjoyed playing baseball in the spring, even though we didn't play too many games. The baseball coach then was Frank Moseley, who was Coach Bryant's No. 1 assistant in football.

Before my sophomore year, we scrimmaged some players, including some former UK stars from Louisville. I guarded

Kenny Rollins, who had been the captain of the "Fabulous Five" in 1948, and he was just too quick for me. I just played poorly. Finally Coach Rupp took me out and said, in that sarcastic way of his, "Go sit down, Newton. You know what you remind me of? A shetland pony in a stud-horse parade." I was really embarrassed. Thank goodness Coach Rupp's practices were usually closed to the public.

I know that Spivey and Frank Ramsey and some of my other former teammates have said that Coach Rupp ruined me as a basketball player because he didn't understand that I was too sensitive to handle his sarcasm and profanity. But I don't quite buy that. The criticism was something where you had to get to the point where it just didn't bother you. Some players were able to overcome it and some weren't. I wanted to please him so badly that it *did* bother me. But it taught me something that was useful to me later: You can't treat everybody the same way. Some players need to be patted on the back and some need to be disciplined. Later, I saw a lot of guys who went into coaching who tried to be like Coach Bryant and Coach Rupp, but they failed. You've got to be yourself. And motivation by fear is not always the best way.

Looking back, I just didn't fit into Coach Rupp's style of play. I would have been better off playing in a less-structured style. Probably the best thing I did was get the ball to other people, and Coach Rupp wanted five guys who could score. So maybe I just wasn't quite good enough. At least I felt I gave it my best shot and I got some playing time for a 25-5 team that got absolutely drilled by City College of New York, 89-50, in the NIT. Our best player was Spivey, a 7-footer from Georgia who was quickly developing into the nation's best big man. When I first saw Spivey at the start of our freshman year, he was skinny as a rail and had very limited basketball skills. But he could run, and after a lot of work with Coach Lancaster, he began to blossom.

My junior year, 1950-51, we moved out of Alumni Gym and into Memorial Coliseum. I remember sitting in history class in Frazee Hall and watching them build it. At the time, it was the biggest on-campus arena in the country, with around 11,500 seats, and some of the critics said we would never fill it on a regular basis. The university also was criticized for spending too much money. As players, the first thing we noticed, other than the incredible size of the place, was the difference in the floor. At Alumni Gym, the floor was built over a basement, so it was soft, with dead spots. But the Coliseum floor was built on concrete, and it was so hard that a lot of us got shin splints.

On Dec. 16, 1950, we played Kansas in the Coliseum. It was a special game for Coach Rupp because it was against his alma mater and his college coach, Phog Allen. (Years later I understood exactly what Coach Rupp was feeling when I coached against him at Alabama and became the only one of his former players to beat him.) Coach Rupp and Coach Lancaster really got Spivey fired up to play against Clyde Lovellette, the 6-9 Kansas All-American. We ripped them, 68-39, mainly because Bill humiliated Lovellette. That game solidified Spivey as the best big man in the country. He was the game's first mobile big man, a giant who could run and jump. He had great basketball skills, particularly the hook shot.

Besides Spivey, we had a couple of great sophomores in Frank Ramsey and Cliff Hagan, who would go on to become members of the Basketball Hall of Fame in Springfield, Mass. Some of the other guys who received a lot of playing time were Watson, Linville and Hirsch. We won the university's third national championship in four years, beating Kansas State, 68-58, in the NCAA title game in Minneapolis and finished with a final record of 32-2. And I'm proud to say that I even made a modest contribution in our 76-74 win over Illinois in the Eastern Regional title game in New York's Madison Square Garden. (There was no Final Four in those days, only East and West regionals that sent the winners to the championship game.)

We got in foul trouble against Illinois, and nobody could stop Don Sunderlage, their star guard. He was just lighting it up. Coach Rupp came down the bench and grabbed me. As he walked me to the scorer's table he said,

"Don't let Sunderlage score ... don't let Sunderlage score ... and for God's sake, don't shoot the ball." Well, I didn't let Sunderlage score. Heck, I almost tackled him once on a fast break. Late in the game, I got an open shot that I passed up because Shelby Linville had broken open. So I passed it to him and we won the game. It felt good to be able to come in and make a contribution in a big game when I was needed. Although I never got to play as much as I wanted, I always felt I was contributing and that I was a part of the team. I could have played more elsewhere, but I wouldn't trade that for my experiences at UK.

They had a parade for us when we got back to Lexington, and as much as I enjoyed it, I knew I had played my final game of basketball for UK. They were starting to give out bonuses in baseball and I wanted to marry Evelyn and end our long-distance courtship. The final straw came after the season, when Coach Rupp told me I couldn't have a basketball scholarship if I got married. I decided then that if I had a decent year in baseball, I'd give up my last year of basketball eligibility.

That summer I pitched a lot of semi-pro baseball with the Eastern Airlines team in Miami. I worked out with the Pirates, who were giving out a lot of big bonuses in those days, and with the Brooklyn Dodgers and the New York Yankees in Yankee Stadium. When it came down to those three, my dad pointed out that the Yankees still hadn't integrated their organization as much as the Dodgers and Pirates. "You may have a better opportunity with the Yankees because you won't have the colored players to compete against," he said. It was the only time I heard anything remotely racist come out of my dad.

Speaking of race, I want to say this about Coach Rupp: He may have been a lot of things, but he wasn't a racist. It really burns me when I read that stuff by some of today's writers. He looked at people as people. One summer I remember him telling us to watch Don Barksdale, a great black player. "Watch his footwork," Coach Rupp would say, admiringly. At the start of the 1951-52 season, St. John's came in to play what would have been my senior year with a black player named Solly Walker. Coach Rupp was concerned about how he would be treated so he wrote a letter to Ed Ashford, the sports editor of *The Lexington Herald*, in which he asked the fans to treat Walker with respect.

Anyhow, my signing with the Yankees had nothing to do with race and everything to do with a $10,000 bonus that I used to pay for my last year of school. They sent me to Norfolk of the Class B Piedmont League, but they were loaded so I finished the season with Muskegon of the Class A Central League. A couple of my teammates were Jim Greengrass and Nino Escalera, who went on to play in the majors for the Cincinnati Reds. Escalera, who was black, was from Puerto Rico and he dressed two lockers away from me. It was no big deal.

I came back to Lexington in September and started school. I lived in the Sigma Alpha Epsilon house, which was a new experience for me. For the first time, I saw college life from a whole different standpoint. I was amazed by how much partying went on. Evelyn and I were planning to get married in December, so she had dropped out of Miami and was working at a bank in Fort Lauderdale. Everything was going great until the October Saturday when I walked into the fraternity house and heard a guy on the radio saying that Ralph Beard and Alex Groza, who were then NBA players with the Indianapolis Olympians, had been picked up in Chicago and charged with shaving points during their UK days. Barnstable, Spivey, Hirsch and Line also were charged. I heard Coach Rupp read his statement — he had earlier bragged that gamblers couldn't touch his players "with a 10-foot pole" — and it was like a dagger through my heart.

This was the first time in my life that people I knew and cared about were in real trouble. I had roomed with Bill Spivey and I never had any inkling that he had any contact with gamblers. I talked with Bill and he looked me right in the eye and said, "I had nothing to do with this." Still, Bill dropped off the team in December, pending the outcome of a university and conference investigation, and he never played again. There's no doubt that the loss of Spivey cost UK the 1952 NCAA championship. And later, even though Bill was tried in New York on perjury charges and had a jury hung 9-3 in his favor, he never was allowed to play in the NBA. That was a tragedy. He was so good that he would have forced the NBA to rewrite the rulebook.

The scandal consumed the community and the Commonwealth. It was so unbelievable and yet so innocent in a lot of ways. A fellow student, a former football player who got the basketball players hooked on going over the point spread, was involved. But nobody will ever convince me that any of our players ever agreed to throw games. On our trips, we were pretty well cordoned off. A lot of people figured that Ed Curd, the bookmaker, was involved because he was a friend of Coach Rupp's. But I never really knew Curd or remember him being around the team. Besides, a bookmaker is the last guy who wants a game fixed. He's already got the edge, so he just wants everything on the up-and-up.

What unfolded in the wake of the scandal changed my life dramatically. I thought I would finish my senior year by doing some student teaching. But then I got a call from Coach Rupp. He said, "Call Harry Stephenson at Transylvania." Harry was Transy's Athletics Director, and he was talking to Walt Hirsch about coaching the basketball team. But when Hirsch was implicated in the scandals, this eliminated him from consideration. Harry told me later that he also wondered about me. But when I called Harry, he said, "I don't have any money to hire you with and you haven't graduated yet, but I need you to coach basketball part-time." And that was how my coaching career began.

Chapter 3
A Special Place Named Transylvania

T hose of us who know and love Transylvania University have learned to grin and bear the Dracula jokes. A liberal-arts school that has an enrollment of around 1,000, Transy is located near the heart of downtown Lexington, not in Romania, and it's the oldest college west of the Allegheny Mountains (it was founded in 1780). Henry Clay, who became known as "The Great Compromiser" during his storied U.S. Senate career in the mid-1800s, was a Transylvania professor. A.B. "Happy" Chandler, who graduated from Transy in 1921, went on to become a U.S. Senator, two-time governor of Kentucky and commissioner of baseball. Still, you mention Transylvania and people give you funny looks. When I went back for a reunion of Alabama players and coaches in August 1999, Robert "Rah Rah" Scott, one of my players and now an Alabama assistant, told the banquet crowd, "To this day, I still don't know where Transylvania is."

When I accepted Harry Stephenson's offer, I inherited a

team that had 12 players, some of whom were older than me. Some of them smoked and weren't real serious about getting into shape. So I talked the older guys into not playing so I could have an age group that I could manage. I put in the Kentucky offense, but then wondered why we couldn't run it very well. As I've said many times, I got my degrees at Kentucky, but my education at Transylvania. I made every mistake you could make with that first team. Once, calling for a Saturday practice during a big campus social weekend, I did my best imitation of Coach Rupp: "Boys, you've got a decision to make — Do you want to be a part of the team or a part of a fraternity?" Well, three guys didn't show up, meaning our roster went from 12 players to nine. That hurt. But it taught me a lesson: Don't put that challenge out there unless you're willing to let it happen.

We played Asbury College in our opener. They played a 2-3 zone the whole game and I had barely practiced against a zone. We ended up getting beat in a game we could have, and should have, won. And so began my on-the-job training as a coach.

On Dec. 22, 1951, right after the first academic quarter, Evelyn and I were married at the Park Temple Methodist Church in Fort Lauderdale. My brother, Richard, couldn't be there because he was in Korea, but my sister, Jean, was one of Evelyn's bridesmaids. For our honeymoon, we went to the

Sugar Bowl basketball tournament in New Orleans. Coach Rupp gave me tickets. I guess that's when Evelyn first realized she might be in trouble as a coach's wife.

Our first home was an apartment on the third floor of Ewing Hall, an ancient building at Transylvania. A friend allowed us to borrow some furniture. We had a big four-poster bed, a card table, a kitchen and a bath. Evelyn got a job at First National Bank and I was finishing up my degree at UK by taking some classes and doing some student teaching. We thought we had it made. The only problem was that we only went 1-15 that season, and the lone victory was against Bellarmine, a new school in Louisville. The program was simply in terrible shape, mainly because Transy didn't give athletic scholarships.

I spent the summer of 1952 pitching for Norfolk of the Piedmont League, then came back to Transy for the 1952-53 academic year. The school had a new president, Dr. Frank Rose, who had been the pastor at the First Christian Church in Danville. Although we still couldn't give athletic scholarships, we actually recruited some players — Bobby Haggard, Al Prewitt, Stoop Adams, Billy Wise — and we had a halfway decent team for being so young. Right after we played in the Kentucky Intercollegiate Athletic Conference Tournament in Owensboro to complete a 5-15 season, I went into the Air Force, where I was commissioned as a lieutenant because of my ROTC experience at UK.

During my two years in the Air Force, I got my first experience as a sports administrator, which I'll discuss later.
I also got one of the biggest jolts of my life when I got a
call in 1955, telling me that Jean had died. Jean was the
spitting image of Mom. She also was a gifted pianist and a
great mother to her only son, Bill Bryan. Mom and Dad ex-
pressed nearly every emotion and spoke often of how difficult it was to lose a child, even when the child had grown
up. My nephew was 15, and suddenly Mom and Dad had a
teenager in the house again. Seeing Mom get through that,
being available for Bill, was really significant for me.

When I came out of the Air Force in the spring of 1955,
I took Evelyn and our daughter Debbie, who had been born
July 10, 1954, to Fort Lauderdale while I went to spring
training. The Washington Senators were trying to buy my
contract at the time, and I was hoping they would because
they needed pitching and the Yankees didn't. They sent me
to Quincy, Ill., of the Class B, Three-I League, where one of
my teammates was an 18-year-old named Tony Kubek, who
went on to become a fine player with the Yankees and then
a network TV analyst. But that summer I knew I would soon
have to make a major career decision. Should I give up
baseball or try it another year? After hauling Evelyn and a
year-old daughter to Quincy, I knew I didn't want to spend
the next several summers in minor-league parks. So what
should I do? The Yankees talked to me about staying in

their system and learning to be a manager, and there was the possibility of going back to Fort Lauderdale and becoming a coach there.

But then Dr. Rose contacted me and said he wanted me to come back to Transy. I told him I would, but only if they began giving athletic scholarships. You just had to have them to compete with Union and Georgetown and the other teams in the KIAC. When he said that was a possibility, I thought, "If you want to coach in college, why not go back there?" Besides, there were other perks. I could get my master's degree at UK on the GI bill. And Transy was essentially a nine-month deal, meaning I could do whatever I wanted in the summers. So Evelyn and I sat down in Quincy after Harry Stephenson had come down to see us and we said, "Let's go back to Transylvania."

My first year back, 1955-56, we practiced and played in the Lexington Junior High gym because Dr. Rose had decided to raise the floor in the old white building that was known as "The Barn" and build McAlister Auditorium around it. He built the library first, then McAlister so he could have convocations and assemblies there. That season we had a 6-8 freshman named LaVern Altemeyer, who was so good he transferred to Illinois after the season, and we claimed the first tournament Transy had won in years, beating Austin Peay, Delta State and David Lipscomb in the Capital City Invitational in Nashville. Our final record was

9-9, the first non-losing season at Transy since 1939-40.

The grants were the key. Dr. Rose had sneaked them past the faculty by calling them "Leadership Grants." Then he came up with something called Lexington Community Scholarships. That's how Harry got Lee Rose there. Harry had offered him $250 per quarter, but he needed more than that. So we got him more money through a Lexington Community Scholarship. He became a really good player for us, and then I hired him as my assistant after he graduated in 1958. He succeeded me when I went to Alabama in 1968 and subsequently had an outstanding coaching career at Transy, UNC Charlotte, Purdue and South Florida.

With the grants, we were able to get better players. I established a good relationship with Lee Gladstein of Scottsburg, Ind., and he helped us get players such as Altemeyer, Jennis "Stick" Stidham, Phil Stewart, Sonny Voyles and Nolan Barger. Our recruiting base was Central Kentucky, Louisville and Southern Indiana. We tried to find promising players who were bypassed by the larger universities because they were late bloomers, and we had some pretty good success with it. Our philosophy was the exact opposite of Georgetown, where Bob Davis recruited a lot of older players who had been in the service or industrial leagues or were transfers from Division I universities.

As our talent got better, we slowly upgraded our schedule. We played teams like Middle Tennessee, Austin Peay and Eastern Kentucky, and we would go to Florida every year to play teams like Stetson and Jacksonville. We got to the point where we were competitive in the KIAC, which was an outstanding basketball league. Pikeville had Donnis Butcher, who went on to play for the Detroit Pistons of the NBA, and Villa Madonna had Larry Staverman, who later played for the Cincinnati Royals. And Georgetown, our arch-rival, had tough players like Dicky Vories, Cecil Tuttle, Bob Jones and many others.

In the fall of 1956, at our first faculty meeting of the year, Dr. Rose surprised everyone by announcing that he was leaving to become president at the University of Alabama. In his short term at Transy, he had raised $1.5 million that he used to get the university out of debt, establish an endowment and build McAlister. Before he left, he told me, "I've got to get the football thing straightened out at Alabama ... I'm going to hire Paul Bryant." I'll always remember that. Dr. Rose was succeeded by Dr. Irvin Lunger, who had been brought in to be Dean of the Chapel. In the early part of Dr. Lunger's administration, Harry had his choice of being athletics director or chairman of the physical education department. He chose to be A.D., so I became the chair. Harry and Mitchell Clark, an English professor, pointed out to me that I was the only chair that didn't have a doctorate, so that's when I began thinking seriously about getting it.

In 1957, Evelyn and I bought our first house on Dellwood Drive. By then, our second daughter, Tracy, had been born. (Our son Martin completed our family in 1961). One night I got an urgent call from the folks about Bill, my sister Jean's son. It just wasn't working, him living with them, so I sat down with Evelyn and asked her what she thought about Bill coming to live with us and finishing up high school. It was a three-bedroom house, so we moved the girls into one bedroom. It was a life-changing experience for Bill and for us, too. It let me have some healing over Jean's death and do something to help the folks out. Bill and I came to have more of a brother relationship. For years he has been one of my best friends and fishing buddies. But the real trooper was Evelyn. I will always be grateful to her for her willingness, at age 26, to become a surrogate mother to a teenager.

Beginning in 1956-57, we had seven consecutive winning seasons. By the start of the 1961-62 season, we were doing so well that Coach Rupp called up one day to say that he wanted to bring some visiting coaches from Japan and other countries over to watch our game with Wittenberg. I was really excited. We put Coach Rupp and his party on the front row at midcourt. At the time, Wittenberg was coached by Ray Mears, who later became Coach Rupp's nemesis at Tennessee, and it was the top-ranked small-college team in the country. Well, Ray liked to play that slowdown brand of basketball that Coach Rupp hated. We beat them in a well-played game, but the score was only 39-38. When a reporter from *The Lexington Leader* asked Coach Rupp how he had liked the game, he said, "Well, I'm glad that C.M. won, but that exhibition set the game of basketball back 50 years." That was Coach Rupp for you.

My best team probably was the 1962-63 bunch that had a 20-9 record and went to the NAIA Tournament in Kansas City, where we lost in the second round. Our leader was Jackie Lucas, a guard who could have played for a lot of major colleges, but we also had an outstanding player in Lynn Stewart, a 6-4 forward who could shoot with range, put the ball on the floor and jump. He was one of those late bloomers we liked to get. Had he stayed in high school another year, Kentucky and those kind of schools would have recruited him. But in the summer of 1963, Lynn and one of his friends decided to go see some girls in Millersburg after a night of drinking at the Buffalo Tavern.

On the way, the car swerved off the highway, and Lynn, who was riding in the passenger's seat, threw up his right arm to protect his face. The arm was severed below the elbow, and they couldn't save it. I was in Florida when Harry called me with the tragic news. That accident was one of the most difficult things I've ever gone through with any young person. Lynn was a difficult player to coach, because he was rather headstrong, and it was even more difficult for him after the accident. Not only was he a very good player, but he was very vain about his looks. He wanted his uniform to fit just right, that sort of thing. It took him a long time to come to terms with the accident. For me, it was another reminder of how alcohol abuse can impact a person's life.

After that season, I got a couple of feelers about jobs at bigger schools. Dr. Adron Doran, the president of Morehead, called me and I went up there to see him. I also got a call from Florida, and being from Florida, I got all excited about that. It came down to me and Norm Sloan, who was at The Citadel then. They picked Norm and, frankly, I was relieved because I wasn't ready to be a coach at that level. But at least I got a new car out of it. Alfred "Petey" Powell, who was one of the greatest supporters Transy ever had, got wind of it and he rounded up some guys to buy me a big ol' Plymouth station wagon.

Looking back, I'd have to say the Transylvania years were the happiest I had in coaching. The unique thing about Transy was its people. The faculty was the most dedicated I ever saw anywhere. Dr. Rose and Dr. Lunger had a major impact on me, as did educators such as Dean Leland Brown and Harry. It was just a great experience all the way around. A family affair. Evelyn and I started our married life there, and our kids grew up in Lexington. I had a full teaching load and was part of the faculty, I ran intramurals and chaperoned social events and I officiated high school games to pick up extra money on Tuesday and Friday nights. The officiating saved Transy all kinds of dollars because I could scout players while I was officiating their games.

I learned how to coach at Transy, and part of it was that there wasn't any external pressure. Oh, we wanted to win and we expected to win, but the external pressure of win-or-else just wasn't there. In the summers, I'd take Evelyn and the kids to Campa Sparta in Sebring, Fla., where I served as camp director. I'd also take some students to work as counselors. A lot of them were players who needed extra work — Bill Brooks of Henry Clay and Larry Langan of Lexington Catholic were a couple of them — and we would work 'em out every day.

In 1964-65, I decided to take a sabbatical from Transy so I could begin working on my doctorate. Alabama was offering a new doctorate in physical education, and all it took was one phone call to Dr. Rose to set me up with a residency. Just as he had told me when he left Transy, in 1958 Dr. Rose talked Coach Bryant into leaving Texas A&M to come to Alabama. By 1961 Coach Bryant had won the first of his five national championships. Hayden Riley, Alabama's basketball coach, called to ask me to coach the freshman team. Dr. Rose had it all greased for me to go down there and not lose any money. Heck, he even let me live in the president's mansion for awhile!

During my absence, Lee Rose took the team over at Transy and did such a fine job that Cincinnati hired him to be its freshman coach. When I came back, I hired Roland Wierwille, who had been a good player for Paul McBrayer at Eastern, to replace Lee. My first year back, we integrated the program with Robert Berry, a 6-6 player from Bryan Station High in Lexington. As I recall, he kind of recruited us in a lot of ways. Like Lynn Stewart and so many others, he was a young kid who needed a lot of development. Although Coach Rupp was under a lot of pressure at UK to integrate his program, we brought in Robert without a lot of fuss. It had already been decided at Transy that we needed as much diversity in the student body as we could get. All that mattered was whether a student was academically qualified. Although Robert never quite panned out as a player, Lee Rose sent us a really good black player named Jim Hurley. Lee had coached him as a freshman at Cincinnati, but they had so much talent they weren't going to give him a scholarship. We were tickled to get him.

After the 1967-68 season, I had a 169-137 record to show for 12 seasons at Transy, and we were in the process of building another team good enough to make a postseason tournament. But one Saturday afternoon that spring, while I was outside taking down storm windows, Evelyn came out and said, "Coach Bryant's on the phone." He mumbled and was hard to understand. I heard him say that Hayden Riley had resigned, and what did I think about the Alabama basketball job? I assumed there would be a committee and he would want me to fly down for an interview.

"Will there be a committee?" I said.

"Hell," said Coach Bryant, "I want to know if you want the job. You discuss it with Evelyn. I'll call you back at 8 o'clock tonight and will answer your questions."

Evelyn and I did a lot of talking in those four hours. She just did not want to leave and go to Alabama because that was a hard time there, with all the integration business. It was a risk leaving the security at Transy, where I had just gotten a raise to $15,500 a year. But I just kept thinking, "What if I would be sitting at Transy five years later wondering what if? How much good would I be then to myself or anybody else?" Plus, I always felt I could go back to a place like Transy because I had proved I could win at that level.

When Coach Bryant called back, I asked him four basic questions. How long a contract would I get? He said four years and I thought that was reasonable. I asked him about the expectations. He said he wanted a good, clean program that was competitive in the SEC. I thought that was reasonable. Then I asked if he would help me establish some contacts and credibility because I was a no-name guy coming in there. He said he would. Finally, I asked if there would be any restrictions on recruiting. What that really meant was, "Can I recruit blacks?" I knew Alabama was integrating its high school programs and I felt we had to recruit the best players in the state, regardless of color. He said there would be no restrictions, except that he wanted good people who could do the academic work. That was good enough for me. I said yes.

The next morning, I came over to McAlister and sat by myself in the stands, waiting for Harry to get out of class. I told him I had been offered the job at Alabama and was going to take it. I also talked to Dr. Lunger and Dr. Jim Broaddus about it. I remember Dr. Lunger saying he was worried I might be too nice a guy to make it in the SEC. "You've got to get tougher," he said. I wasn't worried about that. I always thought that with me, too many people mistook caring for not being tough.

The hardest time we ever had leaving a place was at Transylvania. In talking to Coach Bryant, I never even asked about salary. The contract I ended up signing was for $12,500, and I didn't dare tell Evelyn, who really didn't want to go, that I was asking her to take three children and go to Alabama for $3,000 less than I was making at Transy.

So I went to Alabama. Wimp Sanderson was still around from Hayden Riley's staff, and he and I hit the road right away, recruiting. One night after about a week or so, I couldn't sleep, so I went over to Alabama's new Memorial Coliseum, which then was the biggest in the league with 15,500 seats. I didn't have a key to get in my office so I sat up in the stands. Only the security lights were on.

That's when it dawned on me that I was going to have to put fannies in all those seats. I panicked. I remember thinking, "What in the world have I done?"

C.M. (35) and the Wildcats celebrate a 76-74 victory over Illinois. The win placed UK in the 1951 NCAA title game.

UNIVERSITY OF KENTUCKY

STUDENT
IDENTIFICATION

1950-51

NOTE: This card will be called for on occasions requiring your identification as a student of the University of Kentucky. No alterations are to be made. The card will be confiscated or voided if it is misused. In the event of loss notify the University Registrar, Mr. Lee Sprowles, at once.

CHARLES M. NEWTON
P.O. BOX (UK) 843
LEXINGTON, KY.
DATE OF BIRTH: 2-2-30
HT. 6-2 WT. 193 BROWN HAI

C. M. Newton

C.M. with Harry Stephenson, former athletics director at Transylvania University.

C.M. with (from left) Lee Rose, LaVern Altemeyer and Jimmy Blair.

Above: The 1947-48 Fort Lauderdale High School starting five — Leonce Picot (17), C.M. Newton (10), Steve Powell (12), Wynn Casteel (19), Coach Clois J. Caldwell and Jimmy Fay (top, right).

Adolph Rupp and C.M. prior to a UK-Alabama game.

C.M. leaves the floor following Alabama's 78-64 defeat of Kentucky in Rupp Arena on Jan. 12, 1980.

Lee Gladstein, an early supporter of Transylvania basketball.

Transy supporter Alfred G. "Petey" Powell with former Transylvania President Dr. Irvin Lunger.

C.M. with former UK President Dr. Otis Singletary (center) and former Commissioner of the Southeastern Conference Dr. Boyd McWhorter.

The 1998 NCAA Division I Men's Basketball Committee. Front Row (L-R): Bernard Muir, Rudy Davalos, Terry Holland, C.M. Newton, Charles Harris, Mike Tranghese, Daniel Calandro. Back Row: Bill Hancock, McKinley Boston, Lee Fowler, Craig Thompson, Tom Jernstedt, Carroll Williams, Jim Marchiony.

C.M. with UK equipment manager Bill Keightley.

C.M. is carried off the floor following Alabama's 73-70 defeat of Kentucky in 1972,
the only time a disciple of Rupp ever defeated the Baron.

C.M. with former UK football coach Jerry Claiborne.

Wendell Hudson (far left) and C.M. watch the activities during Wendell Hudson Day.

C.M. with Transy players Jim Hurley, Ronnie Whitson and Nolan Barger.

C.M.'s first senior class at Alabama:
David Mitchell (32), Rich Deppe (33),
Tommy Suitts (10) and Gary Elliott (22).

Wendell Hudson

Coach Bear Bryant and C.M.

Coach Bear Bryant, Coach Adolph Rupp and C.M.

C.M. with the 1964 Transylvania senior class: Dave Yewell (51),
David Jones (50), Virgil Jenkins (13) and Jay Barton (far right).

C.M. and Evelyn form the Y.

Newton family photo (circa 1940). C.M. is seated front and center.

Former UK President Dr. David Roselle welcomes C.M. back as athletics director in 1989.

ATLANTA TIPOFF CLUB

NAISMITH CONTRIBUTION TO BASKETBALL AWARD

C.M. NEWTON
University of Kentucky

Kentucky Athletic Director C.M. Newton

The Atlanta Tipoff Club which presents the Naismith Awards, has named C.M. Newton the 1999 Naismith Outstanding Contribution to Basketball Award winner.

The Atlanta Tipoff Club, now in its 43rd year, established the Naismith Outstanding Contribution to Basketball Award in 1982 in order to honor an individual who has made outstanding contributions to the game and who has been a pioneer of the game. In 1983, the criteria changed to honor a coach who helped develop the great game to its modern popularity. Lifetime achievement and exemplary service are also extremely important measures of the award.

C.M. Newton has been the Director of Athletics at the University of Kentucky since 1989. Before coming to UK, he was the head basketball coach at Transylvania University (1956-68); University of Alabama (1969-1980); Vanderbilt University (1982-89) and Assistant Commissioner, Southeastern Conference (1980-81).

Newton has had a notable basketball coaching career. Two consecutive seasons (1988 and 1989) he was named SEC Coach of the Year and was chosen the 1989 Kodak NABC District IV Coach of the Year. In 32 years he compiled a record of 509-375.

In 1969 Newton answered a call from Paul "Bear" Bryant to take on the challenge of building the Alabama basketball program. In 12 years, Newton managed a complete

turnaround with the Crimson Tide, compiling a 211-123 record. In addition to winning three consecutive SEC championships, there were two trips to the NCAA tournament and four berths in the NIT. The satisfied Bryant once remarked, "C.M. Newton is a winner and that's important, but more than anything else he wins or loses with class, and that's more important."

Newton is highly involved on a national level. He served 11 years on the Board of Directors of the National Association of Basketball Coaches. He worked six years (chaired for five years) on the NCAA Basketball Rules Committee. He was presidnet of USA Basketball, the nation's governing body for all international basketball (1992-1996). He is a member of the NCAA Division I Basketball Committee and became chair in 1997-98. He is also a member of the NCAA Committee on Basketball Issues.

While serving as chairman of the NCAA Men's Basketball Committee, Newton had the pleasure of handing the 1998 championship trophy to Tubby Smith, his handpicked successor to Rick Pitino at Kentucky.

Internationally, he represents North America on the 14-member FIBA Central Board. FIBA is the governing body for international basketball. He is also a member of the COPABA Executive Board which oversees international basketball in North, Central and South America. Newton's international coaching accomplishments include team manager on the 1984 U.S. Olympic team (Gold Medal). He also took Vanderbilt to Taiwan to represent the United States in the R. Williams Jones Cup international tournament, winning the Gold Medal in 1983 and the Silver in 1987.

"C.M. Newton is truly one of the pioneers to our modern game. He is responsible for the innovations that provide the foundations of our great game." Jackie Bradford, Executive Director of the Atlanta Tipoff Club said. "We are proud to honor him with the Naismith Outstanding Contribution Award."

The award will be presented at the Naismith Awards Banquet April 3, 1999 in Atlanta, Ga.

About the Naismith Awards

The Naismith Awards are presented by the Atlanta Tipoff Club located in Atlanta, GA. The first Naismith Award to a college basketball player was given in 1969 when Lew Alcindor (Kareem Abdul-Jabbar) was named as the men's Player of the Year. Since then the awards program has expanded to include women, high school players and contributors to the game of basketball.

C.M. (far left) scouts with George Raveling, Bob Knight and Henry Iba preparing for the 1984 Olympics.

Leon Wood receives some advice from C.M. during the 1984 Olympics in Los Angeles.

To Coach Newton
Best Of Luck!
your friend,

C.M. with Steve Wariner.

Bone fishing partner
and friend Orthnell
Russell with C.M. on
Treasure Cay,
Abaco, Bahamas.

C.M. welcomes new coach Hal Mumme.

RICHLAND COUNTRY CLUB
NASHVILLE, TENN.   AUG. 26, 1983

JUDGE LEWIS CONNER JR
COACH C.M. NEWTON
PRO JOE TAGGERT
GUEST JOCK SUTHERLAND

FOR A REALLY
GREAT DAY!

JOCK

Lewis Conner Jr., C.M., Joe Taggert and Jock Sutherland.

C.M. with administrative support associate Barbara Isham.

(Below) UK Associate AD and Senior Women's Administrator Kathy DeBoer, C.M. and UK Senior Associate AD Larry Ivy.

John McMahon, Rick Pitino and Jim McWane.

C.M. celebrates a victory with former UK football coach Bill Curry.

Chapter 4
Integration and Success at Alabama

I came to Alabama less than five years after George Wallace, then the state's governor, had made his "Stand in the Schoolhouse Door" to prevent the university from becoming integrated. The "schoolhouse" in question was Foster Auditorium, then the university's basketball arena that also was used for registration. The governor's dramatic gesture went for naught, but only after Robert Kennedy, then the U.S. Attorney General, sent in hundreds of National Guardsmen to protect the first black students as they enrolled. As naive as it may sound, I really didn't pay much attention to all this, just as I didn't know until after I had been in Tuscaloosa awhile that Robert Shelton, the Grand Wizard of the Ku Klux Klan, had an office at the end of University Avenue. I was just totally focused on building a basketball program that would be consistently competitive in the Southeastern Conference.

When I took the Alabama job, the SEC was changing dramatically. Kentucky still was the dominant program, of course, but the gap between the Wildcats and the rest of the league was shrinking. For one thing, Coach Rupp was in his 60s and nagged by various health problems. Vanderbilt had broken the color barrier with Perry Wallace in the 1967-68 season. And the league's athletics directors were becoming increasingly aware that basketball was virtually an untapped source of revenue. So most of the SEC schools were building, or planning, new arenas and hiring outstanding coaches. Gone were the days when basketball would be entrusted to an assistant football coach. Ray Mears was making waves at Tennessee, Norm Sloan was doing a good job at Florida and Roy Skinner was continuing his fine work at Vanderbilt.

Everybody had expected Coach Bryant to hire a big-name coach. Some of the names mentioned were Babe McCarthy, who was then coaching the Kentucky Colonels of the ABA, and Frank McGuire, who had built powerful programs at St. John's, North Carolina and South Carolina. Under the circumstances, the only guy who had the guts to hire somebody like me was Coach Bryant. I've never forgotten that. In fact, years later, it had a lot to do with me hiring Hal Mumme of Valdosta State as the Kentucky football coach in 1997.

Naturally, my goals were to reach the point where we could win the SEC championship and play in the NCAA Tournament. At that time, Alabama had never played in the

NCAA or the NIT. Even the famed "Rocket Eight" team of 1955-56, the one that finished 21-3 and went unbeaten in the SEC, didn't play in the postseason. The reason, I suppose, was that the university had an unwritten policy about playing against teams with black players. But Coach Bryant had assured me that times had changed, so I plunged into my new challenge with passion and optimism.

Right away Wimp Sanderson, the only holdover from Hayden Riley's staff, wanted to know if I was going to let him stay. I said, "I don't know, but you're here now, so let's hit the road and start recruiting." So we got on that school plane and salvaged the recruiting year, although we failed to sign either of the black kids we recruited. Henry Harris went to Auburn, and Kansas had Bud Stallworth so tied up that we really didn't have a chance. After recruiting, I got serious about a staff. I brought Joe Hall down from Kentucky, but he turned it down. I decided to keep Wimp because of his experience in the SEC. His willingness to stay on after he had been passed over for the head job showed the kind of person he was. I then hired John Bostick from Gadsden as graduate assistant coach because everybody said he was the best high school coach in Alabama. He cashed in some of his retirement funds and used the G.I. bill to be a part of the staff. Finally, I talked Jock Sutherland into leaving Lafayette High School in Lexington because I knew he was a good teacher and had the personality to be a good recruiter.

We were hired to turn the program around and we turned it around immediately. Hayden Riley had gone 10-16 the previous year. Our record was 4-20 overall and 0-10 on the road. You can imagine how popular we were, considering that I was a no-name coach to begin with. But Coach Bryant did something for which I'll always be grateful. We had just lost three straight overtime games — to Kentucky, Mississippi State and Ole Miss — and I was pretty frustrated. When we got home from Ole Miss, instead of going home, I came into the office to study film and see what we could have done differently. At 6 a.m., Coach Bryant stuck his head in my office. He must have heard the projector running. "C.M., I'd like to see you when you're through," he said. My first thought was: Surely he's not going to fire me in the first year. So I went to see him and he said, "I've been through this and I know you're second-guessing yourself. That's of no value. Get away from it some. Go home and see your family." That gave me another mentor and opened the door for me to go to him over the years with a lot of personal and professional things. I really needed that at that time. It taught me the value of having an athletics director who had coached.

During that horrible first year, we made a major breakthrough when Wendell Hudson of Parker High in Birmingham agreed to become the first black scholarship athlete in the university's history. We first noticed Wendell when we went to see one of his teammates, Alvin McGrew, an outstanding guard who also was a very fine baseball player. However, I couldn't get my eyes off Wendell. He was skinny as a rail, but he could really play. Although it was indicated to us that McGrew would play baseball, we kept going back to see him every Tuesday and Friday — and every time Wendell impressed us. I remember vividly a staff meeting where I asked who else was recruiting him. The answer was Miles College and some junior college in Mississippi. That's where you get scared. Auburn had already told him he wasn't strong enough to play in the SEC. All the things you would want in your first black player, where everybody would look at him and say "Wow!," he didn't fit the bill. But I finally said, "They're going to fire us if we don't get it done, so let's at least do it the way we want to do it ... It's the right thing to do, so let's do it." I just knew that Wendell's mother was a very strong person, that everybody we talked to couldn't say enough good things about him, and that he wanted to come. So he would either show us that he could play or that we couldn't judge talent, one or the other.

We didn't want it to be a circus signing, and it wasn't. I think only three newspaper writers and a photographer were there. We didn't have TV and all that stuff. Mrs. Hudson served us Kool-Aid and doughnuts. I remember Mrs. Hudson asking me, "What's it going to be like for my boy at Alabama?" I told her, "I don't know. All I know is how I will treat him and how our staff will treat him. He will be treated no differently than anybody else. We will be fair. We just want him to be the best basketball player and citizen he can be, and we want him to graduate."

Looking back, the key to the whole thing at Alabama was Wendell. I've gotten a lot of credit over the years for integrating the Alabama program and the SEC. I've even been called courageous. But it didn't take any courage on my part. However, it took tremendous courage on Wendell's part. He was the only black person living in Bryant Hall, the athletics dorm. I'm sure Coach Bryant talked to his football players about accepting Wendell. Still, it had to be very lonely for him at times. He just showed tremendous courage.

Under the NCAA rules in effect in those days, freshmen couldn't play on the varsity, so Wendell played on our freshman team. There were some ugly incidents when the freshmen played on the road. The worst was at Auburn, when some football players sat right behind our bench and said some stuff to Wendell that was just unbelievable. I went to Lee Hayley, then the Auburn A.D., and he stopped that in a hurry. I remember another time when Wendell had been treated roughly at Ole Miss. When we crossed the state line back into Alabama, Wendell asked us to stop the bus. I thought he was sick. Instead, he got out, got on his knees, and kissed the ground. "I've never been so happy to be back in Alabama," he said. Our players cracked up.

During Wendell's freshman year, our varsity improved to 8-18, but we also signed two more black players from the state — Raymond Odums and Ernest Odom. Still, I told our coaches that if they were offered a decent opportunity to go elsewhere, they might want to think about it because we could get fired if I couldn't get it done. That's when Jock left to go back to Lafayette High in Lexington. I moved John Bostick to the full-time position and brought in Tommy Suitts, who had been on my first Alabama team, as the graduate assistant. Well, when Wendell joined the varsity in 1970-71, we were 6-6 and on the brink of being a decent team when he broke his wrist going for a rebound in the opening minutes of our Tennessee game at home, putting him out for the season. That was the year when the local paper really started yipping at me. It was my third year and their attitude was, "Same old, same old."

One day Coach Bryant came into my office and asked, "Where do you think the program is?" I told him I thought we were on the verge of getting it turned around, that we were right there. He said, "I do too, and I want to renew your contract." When he called the press conference to announce it, all the guff stopped and that gave us a chance to succeed. Had he not done that, we might not have gotten Charles Cleveland, a 6-6 player who really was a key guy for us.

With Wendell healthy as a junior in 1971-72, we had a breakthrough season. We finished 18-8, the school's best record since the "Rocket Eight," and I was named SEC Coach of the Year. Late in the season, we defeated Kentucky, 73-70, at home, enabling me to be the first of Coach Rupp's former players to beat him. It was big, and our players made it even bigger by picking me up and carrying me off the floor. After the game, Coach Rupp said, "You deserved to win the game ... your boys played well." For a brief instant, I felt that finally he was talking to me as an equal, coach-to-coach. That was important to me because all my coaching life I had wanted Coach Rupp to accept me as a peer. But that only lasted a couple of seconds. Then he said, "Newton, you've got to simplify your offense — you're trying to do too much." Just like that, the cloud vanished. I was back to being one of his boys again. But I never worried about it after that. At the end of that year, UK forced Coach Rupp to retire and, when he came down to speak at our banquet, he was very bitter about it.

At halftime of that Kentucky game, we introduced Leon Douglas, a 6-9 youngster who we desperately wanted. The students chanted, spontaneously, "We want Leon, we want Leon." Coach Bryant spoke at Leon's postseason banquet and that helped him as well as us, considering that a tight end named Ozzie Newsome was an underclassman at Leon's high school. When we got Leon, it was the final piece of the puzzle. He was the kind of strong pivotman who could take the program from being good to being really good. Leon came in before the program was established, and players such as T.R. Dunn, Anthony Murray, Rickey Brown, Reginald King, Robert Scott and many others followed.

In 1972-73, we became the first SEC school to start four black players. We had Leon at center as a freshman (the NCAA had changed its rules and made freshmen eligible for the varsity), Wendell Hudson at forward and Charles Cleveland and Ray Odums at the guards. Until then, the un-written rule was that no one in the SEC would start more than two blacks. Well, we shot the heck out of that quota thing. By the time we started five black athletes a year or two later, all that quota business was dead and gone. We finished second in the SEC with a 13-5 record and accepted an invitation to play in the NIT, the school's first postsea-son appearance. We made it to the semifinals in New York's Madison Square Garden and lost to eventual champion Virginia Tech, 74-73. Much to my pleasure, Wendell was named the SEC Player of the Year.

In 1973-74, we won our first SEC title with a 15-3 league record, and our 22-4 overall record was more than enough to make the NCAA Tournament field. However, there was a rule that stipulated only one school from each conference could enter the 25-team NCAA field. Although Vanderbilt matched our 15-3 SEC record, the Commodores advanced to NCAA play by virtue of their two hard-fought regular-season triumphs over Alabama (73-72 in Nashville, 67-65 in Tuscaloosa). So we sat home and watched some teams that weren't as good as us play NCAA games — in our building nonetheless. Let me tell you, that was hard to take.

The next year we had a really good team. We finished the regular season at 22-3 and won the league for the second straight year. Two of our losses came to Kentucky, which advanced to the NCAA title game before losing to Coach John Wooden's last UCLA team. We received Alabama's first NCAA Tournament bid and were sent to the West Regional to play a good Arizona State team led by future NBA star Lionel Hollins. Although we lost, 97-94, I felt our program had arrived at the point where we could compete against anybody in the country.

The 1975-76 team was the only one I coached that I thought was good enough to win the national championship. The starters were Leon at center as a senior, Reggie King and Rickey Brown at forwards, and T.R. Dunn and Anthony Murray at the guards. In the regular season, we had a 22-4 record and won our third consecutive SEC championship. Sent to the first round of the NCAA Mideast Regional in Dayton, Ohio, we absolutely drilled a great North Carolina team (79-64) that had four starters headed for the NBA (Walter Davis, Tom LaGarde, Mitch Kupchak and Phil Ford). Leon, with 35 points and 17 rebounds, was simply magnificent. That earned us the right to advance to the regional semifinals in Baton Rouge, La., where we were matched against Coach Bob Knight's unbeaten, top-ranked Indiana Hoosiers.

Bob and I had been friends for years. We knew each other from clinics and we usually talked about basketball, not tax shelters or shoe contracts or the stuff that concerns many coaches today. I remember that once, sitting next to each other on a plane, we talked about how we would play each other.

"How would you defend the screens in our motion offense?" he asked me.

"I'd run right through your screens," I said, "and just put the burden on the officials. I think half your screens are illegal, anyway. We'd just have some of the damnedest collisions you ever saw."

Then I asked him how he would defend our offense.

"I'd let you enter the ball to the wing," he said, "but I would not let you reverse the ball. I would keep the ball on one side of the court by playing great pressure and overplay. Your strength is when you reverse-action the ball."

Before we played Indiana, we went into our smaller practice gym because I didn't want anybody to see our preparations. I had so much respect for Bob's pressure man-to-man defense that we practiced our offense against six defensive players. Our guys were of the mindset that we're going to see this great Indiana pressure, so we start the game and they play five guys packed around Leon inside the paint. For a while I didn't know if we were ever going to score. But once we got past that point, we were all right and it turned out to be a great game.

The pivotal play was a charge-block call late in the second half. Their center, Kent Benson, was driving and Leon set himself for the charge. One official set up to call charge, which would have been Benson's fifth foul. Without Benson, I really liked our chances. Instead, however, Leon was called for blocking, his fourth foul. They won, 74-69, and that turned out to be their toughest test on the way to the first of Bob's three NCAA titles. Over the years, Bob has said many times that our '76 team was one of the best he ever coached against. The way we played, from a team standpoint, was really exceptional. We just happened to run into an Indiana team that ranks with UK's "Fabulous Five" as one of the best college teams I ever saw play. Had we gotten past Indiana, I don't think anybody else could have beaten us.

At that point we really had it going and we stayed good the rest of my time at Alabama. In 1977-78, I had my first experience with drug usage on a team. I found out through a student newspaper guy that some of our best players were using marijuana. I knew what that would do to the morale of the team, and I knew it was illegal, so I gave them a choice of leaving the team or accepting a redshirt year with mandatory counseling. In retrospect, I wouldn't have protected the players the way I did in dealing with the media. There should have been some public accountability.

Some interesting things happened in 1978-79, when we had a 22-11 record and finished third in the league. By this time Dale Brown, who had replaced Press Maravich at LSU, really had his program going. Dale and I were natural antagonists because we had such different personalities and probably because we were both competing for SEC championships. In his early years, he was involved in one scrape or another at different places in the league. But Dale and I got along very well until we played them in Baton Rouge in late February.

With 38 seconds to go, they had the game wrapped up. But then Dale called a timeout out so he could order a purple-and-gold banner dropped from the ceiling. The banner proclaimed them to be the 1979 SEC regular-season champion, and their crowd went nuts. Well, I resented that. We had won three SEC titles without embarrassing anybody. I thought it was totally inappropriate. So I charged up to Burl Crowell, one of the officials, and I said, "If you don't get this game started before I get back to the bench, we're leaving the floor and you'll have to finish the game without us. We're not going to participate in their damn celebration." Well, Burl got the game started again and we finished it. Later on, it only made me madder when Dale said that "it was not done in poor taste." Regardless, we have put this incident behind us now and maintain a relationship based on mutual respect.

That season the SEC Tournament was revived. When we met UK in the semifinals, the result was a classic that people still ask me about every now and then. In his last SEC game at Alabama, Reggie King was fabulous, scoring 38 points. But Kentucky won, 101-100, because it shot better than 70 percent from the field. Their guards, Kyle Macy and Truman Claytor, were 20 of 30. As I told the media afterward, "There's no defense for a 25-footer."

We went to the NIT and advanced to the semifinals in Madison Square Garden. There, as fate would have it, our opponent was Purdue, coached by Lee Rose, who had played and coached for me at Transylvania. We couldn't do anything with Joe Barry Carroll, their talented 7-foot center, and they beat us, 87-68. It was the first time I had lost to one of my former pupils, so I understood a little bit what Coach Rupp must have felt like when he lost to me.

In 1979-80, my last year in Tuscaloosa, we had a young team. We finished a respectable 18-12 and again went to the NIT, where we were upset by Murray State. But during the season, for the first time, I started hearing from people I thought were supporters that we had too many black players. It wasn't anybody who mattered, but it was bothersome to me. I thought, "With all we've accomplished, aren't we past that?" The other thing that bothered me was the decline in support. I had felt all along that if we did our part, we would develop the fan base. But there was a perception that we weren't very good that year — we got off to a 5-6 start — and we couldn't overcome that.

So we beat LSU and Kentucky on the road and our players were really excited about going home to play Georgia. It was a rainy night, I'll admit that, but I'll bet there weren't 6,000 fans in our place. You could just see the excitement draining out of our players and it really made me furious. So after the game, which we lost 68-65, I did something by design. Usually, on my postgame radio show, I wasn't very colorful. Bland, to be honest about it. But on this night, when I was asked to discuss the game, I just said I had something else to talk about. And I went into it. I said the program was appreciated more away from Tuscaloosa than it was in Tuscaloosa. I just really drilled it, on and on.

When I got home that night, I told Evelyn that I thought it was really time for me to leave Alabama. That maybe it was time for somebody else to come in and try to take it to the next level. She reminded me of the saying, "It's always best to leave when you're still in love." The next morning, Sam Bailey, an assistant A.D., jumped me for popping off on the radio. I told him things were bothering me that I knew shouldn't bother me. After that I had a series of talks with Coach Bryant, who mentored me through the whole thing. I told him I wanted to take a serious look at some administrative jobs I was interested in. I had been approached about the Florida State A.D.'s job and I had talked with Dr. Boyd McWhorter, the commissioner of the SEC, and Dr. Otis Singletary, the UK president who also was president of the SEC, about joining the league office. Coach Bryant reminded me of the saying, "If you're a CPA, never make a career decision on April 16." I knew what he was saying. Don't act out of exhaustion or frustration. But I was 50 years old and I thought I had accomplished everything I wanted to accomplish in coaching. So I decided to take the job in the SEC office, even though I took quite a reduction in salary — more than half, in fact. The university announced my resignation and Wimp's hiring in one fell swoop. I recommended him. He deserved it and he was the logical guy.

The 12 years we spent in Tuscaloosa were not easy in many ways. When you go 4-20 and you've integrated the program, you're not very popular. I wasn't aware of the stress it put on my family in the early years, especially Debbie, my older daughter, who was just entering high school and having to listen to all this stuff about her dad. But it's also true that the Alabama era meant everything to me. It established me in a national setting as somebody who could coach basketball. Maybe not a great coach, but a good coach. That did a lot for my self-esteem, doing something that people said you couldn't do. I take great pride, not only that we won games and championships with players who were mainly from Alabama, but that we graduated our players. I just regret that Dad, who died in 1967 while we were at Transylvania, didn't live to see what we did at Alabama. At least Mom, who came to live with us after we moved to Tuscaloosa, was there in the early years.

When I left Alabama, I was sure my coaching career was over.

Chapter 5
Change Was Dandy,
But Here Came Vandy

When it was announced that we were leaving Alabama, some of my friends wanted to do something for me, but I wouldn't let them. I said that whatever they did, it should be done around the basketball banquet instead of having a separate function. They had previously given me a fishing boat with a motor that could be put on the back of a houseboat. That was perfect because Evelyn and I wanted to do some things together that we hadn't been able to do. I looked at 50 as a sort of magical age, the right time to make a career move. I felt like I'd really had enough coaching and had prepared myself to do other things, such as being the commissioner of the SEC or another major conference.

One thing that's really tough about leaving a coaching job is that your decision also affects the lives of your assistant coaches and their families. I asked Wimp to retain John Bostick and my other assistant, Leroy McClendon, for at least a year, and he readily agreed. When we left

Tuscaloosa, I rented my house in Woodland Hills to Leroy. That's kind of funny when I think about it now. After integrating the Alabama program, my last act in Tuscaloosa was integrating the neighborhood.

In my last years at Alabama, I was making decent money for the first time. Not the big, big money that a lot of coaches get today. But I was making something in the neighborhood of $90,000, and I took the job in the league office for $42,000. I told Evelyn, "If we're going to take this job in administration, we've got to cut back financially." But that didn't bother me because I've seen too many people pass up an interesting career change just because of money. The most important elements in career changes are the timing has to be perfect, and you've got to have a willingness to risk income and failure. You've got to be willing to go backwards financially to go forward professionally. So we bit the bullet. We moved from a five-bedroom home on $1\frac{1}{2}$ acres with a pond to a two-bedroom condominium in Birmingham.

I suppose my interest in a career in sports administration goes back to my Air Force career. In those days, there was intense athletic competition between the services and the bases. I remember the Army had a strong baseball team at Fort Lee because they were able to get Harry Chiti, a catcher for the Chicago Cubs, and a young outfielder for the New York Giants named Willie Mays. When I arrived at Lackland

Air Force Base in Texas, Bobby Watson, who had been one of my teammates at Kentucky, told me, "Newt, we're going to get you to come to Andrews Air Force Base to play basketball and baseball." Gen. E. Blair Garland had decided he wanted to have strong athletic teams at Andrews.

John Toomay was the coach at Andrews and I was the playing assistant. We put in the Kentucky offense and I started at guard. The Fort Belvoir Army Base had a very strong team that included Dick Groat, the All-American from Duke and eventual star shortstop with the Pittsburgh Pirates. The Quantico Marine Base, the champions of their branch of the service, had Paul Arizin of Villanova and Richie Regan of Seton Hall. But we had Cliff Hagan and Lou Tsioropoulos, who had led Kentucky to a 25-0 record in 1953-54, and we won the Air Force and Inter-Service championships two years in a row.

One day I got a call from Col. Bland, the base commander, who informed me I would become the Base Athletics Officer, a new position he was creating. He wanted to build a strong intramurals program, and part of the reason was to cut down on the off-base incidents of rowdiness by giving the men an outlet for their aggressiveness and to fill their leisure time. I had an almost unlimited budget and the total freedom to build a strong intramural program. So we built a softball field, a baseball field and a nine-hole golf course. We also played host to the worldwide Air Force boxing championships.

I was in charge of all the scheduling for our basketball and baseball teams. We played college teams such as Maryland, Richmond, Georgetown and George Washington. We toured with the Minneapolis Lakers in Kentucky one year, and we went to Lexington and practiced against Kentucky. It was a great experience for me, the best possible on-the-job training to become an athletics director. I even thought about staying in the Air Force, but I wanted to see how my baseball career played out.

With that positive experience in my background, I went to work for the SEC as an associate commissioner, assuming Cliff Harper's responsibility of overseeing basketball operations. That meant dealing with scheduling, officiating, the SEC Tournament, television — everything to do with basketball. But Dr. H. Boyd McWhorter also didn't want me to be pigeon-holed, so he threw other things at me to help prepare me for a career in administration. One of them was that I became the SEC's liaison with the NCAA. That's how I came to spend a day in Kansas City with Walter Byers, the man who essentially invented the modern NCAA. He was just a fascinating man, and I learned a lot from him in that one day. It also was a time when I met a young NCAA staff person named Tom Jernstedt, an individual that I'll discuss more later.

As I was plunging into all this, Dr. McWhorter said something that has stuck with me to this day. "You can give up income and give up being on a college campus," he said, "but the greatest thing you're going to give up is the luxury of being biased." As a coach, all I had to do was support the Transylvania Pioneers or the Alabama Crimson Tide. But as a league administrator, all members are your teams. It's hard, but at that level it's essential. That first year, I had a couple of nice tests to see if I could do it. There was a problem involving Kentucky, my alma mater, and Ole Miss. And there was another situation involving Wimp. But I put my personal feelings aside and resolved them as fairly as I possibly could.

For the first time in my life I had a regular job. I'd go to work at 8:00 in the morning and be home at 4:30 or 5:00. I had to do some traveling, but it was traveling that I could control. After awhile, Evelyn reminded me of that old joke: I married you for better or for worse, but not for lunch. Truthfully, though, it was a nice time for us. Martin was there in Birmingham, playing for Samford as their starting point guard, so we got to watch his games. Evelyn and I had more freedom than we'd had in our years together, and I was all set to go back and do the work necessary to finish my doctorate.

As for the job, it really stretched me from the standpoint of giving me a lot of new, different ways to view college athletics. I'd always been on a campus and had never looked at things from the NCAA standpoint or the conference standpoint. The other thing that I found out, and it came in subtle and different ways, was that it wasn't coaching that I was tired of — it was coaching at Alabama. I don't know how to explain that. Maybe I had come to feel the way Coach Bryant had when he left Kentucky — I realized that no matter what I did, my sport would never be fully appreciated by the Alabama people. When we were winning conference championships, Coach Bryant was winning national championships. I knew I had done all I could do at Alabama. I had no thought of going back to coaching when I went to work for the SEC. My aim was to become the commissioner of the SEC or another major conference.

But I also began to feel a little tug as I traveled around the league, watching games and practices. I'd coached against everybody in that league, but I was never able to see anybody's practices but my own. That was a real eye-opener for me because so many coaches were totally different from what I had thought. There were some who I viewed as hard workers who really didn't work that hard. And some who I thought were always totally prepared who really weren't. It just taught me that there are a lot of ways to coach basketball.

When the 1981 SEC Tournament was held in Birmingham I was the tournament manager. In the first round, Vanderbilt, coached by Richard Schmidt, upset Kentucky, 60-55. Schmidt had coached at Ballard High School in Louisville in the 1970s and early '80s, turning out such fine Division I players as Jeff Lamp and Lee Raker, who played on Virginia's 1981 NCAA Final Four team, and Jerry Eaves, a starter on Louisville's 1980 national championship team. But the rumor mill had it that he was fighting to save his job. After the win over Kentucky, I ran into Roy Kramer, then Vanderbilt's athletics director, in a hallway at the Civic Center. He said, "I'd like to have a few moments, at some point, to talk with you."

So I invited him to the condominium so we could have some privacy and visit. Soon after we sat down he said, "I've decided to make a coaching change ... Would you consider being our basketball coach?" That really shocked me. Since leaving Alabama, I'd had four or five feelers from different places, and it was easy for me to say, "No way." But this time I said, "I might ... I need to think about it."

Even before I talked with Evelyn, I bounced it off John McMahon, a good friend in Birmingham and a very ethical guy. He said, "It's a great school, and you're too good a coach to retire at such a young age." Then I asked Evelyn what she thought. It surprised her, but I saw the same excitement in her that I was feeling. She had always liked Nashville. Then I talked to Dr. McWhorter, and he said he understood completely. Before becoming the SEC commissioner, he had been dean of the College of Arts & Sciences at Georgia. He was truly an academician, but he really understood the relationship between athletics and higher education. Most of all, he had more common sense than almost anybody I had ever been around.

By the time we snuck into Nashville, Roy already had relieved Schmidt. We stayed at the Opryland Hotel. Evelyn and I toured the facilities and then talked some more. "This is something I'd really like to do," I told her, "and this will be our last move." The more I thought about it, the more it seemed like the natural thing to do. Unlike Alabama, Vanderbilt was a place where basketball was appreciated and important. The program had tradition — Bob Polk and Roy Skinner had coached some fine teams there in the 1950s, '60s and '70s — and it had a great fan base. It also was unlike Alabama in that I wouldn't be going in there as "C.M. who?" We had competed against them and they'd seen my teams play. And then there was the academic side of it. Here you had a school that wanted to compete in athletics without lowering the bar academically. To me, it was like a bigger Transylvania. Finally, I trusted and respected Roy Kramer. He had coached and he knew what we needed in order to be successful. It just seemed to be a good fit for me.

I talked to Wimp and told him that I wanted to talk to John Bostick about joining me, if I decided to take the job. I told John, "I'm not sure I'll go if you don't go with me."

I just felt like I needed somebody really strong with me. He said, "Let's go!" When I met with Roy, I told him I wouldn't negotiate dollars. "You give me your best shot and I'll give you yes or no," I told him. Well, his best shot was doggoned good. For the first time, I would be making significant dollars. So I took the job with the attitude that we would go and enjoy it until whenever they told me I couldn't coach anymore. Then we would retire.

When the announcement was made, the Vanderbilt people seemed delighted that I was coming there to coach. But the Alabama people were shocked. There was never anything overt about it, but I felt there was resentment beneath the surface. Now I would be competing against them. People like Coach Bryant and Sam Bailey treated me just the same, but it was never really the same with Wimp. I understood that. I had become a competitor. It was an unusual situation, moving to another school in the same league. But it seemed that when I went to Vanderbilt, Wimp and some of the other people at Alabama tried to forget the 12 years I had spent there. They would honor the guys who preceded my era and the guys who came after that, but there just wasn't much mention of the guys who played for me. That wasn't really rectified until Mark Gottfried had a reunion of Alabama players in August 1999. It was something that was sorely needed, and a lot of healing was done that weekend.

I inherited a young team, and I was lucky to get Phil Cox of Cawood, Ky., as my first recruit. Over the years, Vanderbilt had benefitted greatly from Kentucky players that the Wildcats didn't want. I'm talking about guys like Keith Thomas, Bob "Snake" Grace, Kenny Gibbs and Tommy Hagan. Cox was something special, a great shooter and leader, and I should have kept on trying to recruit players like him. But I made the mistake of trying to recruit people we had no chance to get. I guess I thought if Duke and Stanford could do it, so could we. I said I didn't want to recruit anybody who wasn't a top 100 prospect, but we didn't get a single one. I made some very poor recruiting decisions that got us in a pickle.

I learned that you've got to know who you are and what you can, or can't do. Vanderbilt was not perceived as a national university, at least in basketball. The ACC was perceived to be a better basketball conference, and Stanford was perceived to be more diversified and better academically. So after learning the hard way for a couple of years, I went back to what I did at Transylvania — looking for players who would be late-bloomers. We would try to identify these kind of prospects early and project them as seniors. We hoped to get in with them ahead of Kentucky and the other high-profile programs.

In 1981-82, my first season, we went 15-13. The fans and the media seemed happy and patient. But behind the scenes, we discovered that Evelyn had lymphoma. One night we were out to dinner with a physician. He noticed a growth on Evelyn's neck and told her she ought to have it biopsied. As it turned out, she was assigned to an oncologist at Vanderbilt who specialized in that field. Had we still been in Tuscaloosa or Birmingham, we probably would have gotten somebody who would have treated it very aggressively. But he treated it the right way, and Evelyn responded positively. I guess it was just being in the right place at the right time.

It was also that first year when Roy Kramer called me one day and said, "My diving coach just quit ... do you think Evelyn can help us out?" She had never coached diving at the college level, only the summers we spent at Camp Sparta, but she thought this was something she would like to try. So she became the diving coach for both the Vanderbilt men's and women's teams. She did it for a few years and she was good at it, too.

I got a chuckle before her first meet.

She always had insisted that our home was our home, and that I shouldn't bring my coaching problems into it with me. She always said, "It's only a game, there are more important things to life than basketball." So here she was, down on the pool deck before that first meet, all clammy and glassy-eyed. I couldn't resist going up to her and saying, "Hey, it's only a game." And she said, "Like heck, it's only a game!"

We sent her off on her first recruiting trip without knowledge of the NCAA rules, and that led me to become the first husband in the history of college sports to report his wife for a recruiting violation. She called me from the YMCA Nationals at Fort Lauderdale and said, "I've found a really good female diver from Cincinnati named Patti Woodcock, and her family is just wonderful." I asked her if she had made any contact with them at the site, which would be a rules violation. "I've been sitting with them and last night I had dinner with them," she said. And then I said, "Don't tell me you paid for the meal." But, of course, she had.

So I went to Roy and said, "We may have a problem with our diving coach." I told him what had happened and he told me to write it up for submission to the SEC office. I said, "Why don't you let me call Dr. McWhorter and report this thing?" So I did and Dr. McWhorter said, "She did *what?*" But then he told me to sit Evelyn down and be sure she understood the rules. He said the league would treat it as a secondary violation and file it away. It would only be a problem if there was a repeat violation. This was an example of his great common sense.

When I explained the rules to Evelyn, she said, "Well, that's a dumb rule." And I replied, "Yeah, there are a lot of dumb rules." But she never broke another one during the rest of her career, at least as far as I know.

Despite the lymphoma, Evelyn was really enjoying our new life. She wanted to get her teeth straightened so one day she came home and had braces on. Then she told me she had talked to a professor and was going to take piano lessons. "Evelyn," I said, "you've got this all backwards. You're supposed to have braces and take piano lessons when you're an adolescent, not at age 50." But she was happy and that made me happy.

Our second season we jumped to 19-14 and earned a bid to the NIT, where we lost to Wake Forest in the second round. So far, so good. But by the 1983-84 season, my recruiting mistakes were starting to kick in. We dropped to 14-15 with a team led by Cox, then a junior, and Jeff Turner, a 6-9 senior center who led us in scoring and rebounding. Phil and Jeff were real bellwethers for us.

But nobody was panicking and, just as I had hoped, I felt at home at Vanderbilt. It was at this time, the spring and summer of 1984, that I had one of the most enjoyable and interesting experiences of my coaching career. I packed my bags and headed to Bloomington, Ind., to help Bob Knight select and coach the U.S. team that would compete in the Olympic Games in Los Angeles.

Chapter 6
Going for the Gold with
Bob and Michael

One day at our Olympic team's practice in Indiana University's Assembly Hall, we were working on attacking zones. Our head coach, IU's Bob Knight, said, "A lot of you have been taught to not dribble against a zone, but you've got to dribble-penetrate to distort a zone and we're going to practice that." So the ball goes to Michael Jordan, who soon was to leave North Carolina after his junior year to play in the NBA. He penetrates and hangs in the air, getting two defenders to come to him, and then passes it off.

"Michael," Bob yelled, "don't leave your feet."

So then we start again and Michael does the same thing. He goes up and just sort of hangs there, looking around awhile, until he passes. So now Bob turns up the volume. Now it's, "Michael! Don't leave your feet! Stay on the floor!"

Well, the third time Michael does the same thing and dumps it down low for a bucket. Bob is furious. But before he could say anything, I said, "He's just going to stay up in the air until somebody gets open ... let's not screw him up."

And we didn't.

In fact, we didn't screw anything up during the 1984 Olympics. It was the most efficient and best organized thing of its kind that I was ever involved with, and it was mostly because of Bob. He was tireless in his efforts to win the gold medal in only the second summer Olympics held on U.S. soil. Bob was great throughout the Olympics, as we knew he would be. He's a patriot who loved representing the United States and he wanted to do it right.

Although my interest in international basketball began in 1948, when Kentucky's "Fabulous Five" comprised most of the team that won the Olympic gold medal in London, I didn't get involved as a coach until the late 1970s, when I took a couple of my Alabama teams to Japan and Guatemala. The thing I noticed most was that the globe was shrinking, at least in terms of basketball. As the game's popularity grew, the foreign players and coaches were getting better every year. We first saw this in 1972, when our men's team lost to the Russians in the Munich Olympics, the first time we had failed to win the gold medal. Although most observers felt we were victims of horrible officiating, the most salient point was that the Russians were good enough to take us to the limit. We reclaimed the gold in Montreal in 1976 with a team coached by North Carolina's Dean Smith. But in 1980, when my good friend Dave Gavitt of Providence was to coach the U.S. team, our government decided to boycott the Moscow Olympics to protest Russia's invasion of Afghanistan.

During the 1980-84 period, I was chairman of the staff selection subcommittee for the ABAUSA (Amateur Basketball Association of the United States of America), which later evolved into USA Basketball. We selected the staffs for competitions such as the Olympic Festival, the U.S. Juniors, the World Championships and the Pan American Games. Everything we did during that period was geared toward the 1984 Olympic Games in Los Angeles. In the summer of 1982, for example, I took a United States select team to Geneva, Switzerland, for the 50th Federation of International Basketball Associations tournament. Our starting guards were Michael Jordan and Notre Dame's John Paxson, who later had a pretty good run with the Chicago Bulls. We toured through Yugoslavia before we came home. I really enjoyed putting that kind of team together and taking them out of the country to see how they would respond and react, always with the Olympics in the back of my mind.

We decided that we wanted to pick the 1984 Olympic coach earlier than usual so that he could pick his staff and have input into the last two years of planning. The name at the top of the list was Bob Knight, who had coached NCAA championship teams in 1976 and 1981. Although nobody could question Bob's coaching credentials, there was considerable discussion about what happened at the 1979 Pan-Am Games in Puerto Rico. During a practice, Bob had gotten into an altercation with a Puerto Rican policeman. He was arrested and detained briefly. Had it been another coach in another sport, it would have been no big deal. But because it was Bob, it became an international incident. Most of the U.S. media roasted him as an "ugly American" and worse. Because of that, there was some thought that Bob shouldn't be the 1984 Olympic coach. However, as we discussed various names, Bob emerged as the strongest candidate. By the time we were through, it was almost unanimous. Bryce Durbin, the president of ABAUSA, and I called him with the news. He was excited and immediately went to work on picking his staff.

The Olympic staff consists of the head coach, two assistants and the team manager, who's responsible for all administrative duties. Bob selected Don Donoher of Dayton and George Raveling, who was then at Iowa, to be the assistants. He then asked me to be the team manager because of my administrative experience and because he wanted another coach to fill that role. I was very excited. I had seen what the Olympic gold medal had meant to Ralph Beard and those Kentucky guys in 1948. Plus, anytime you're asked to represent your country, it's an honor. My boss at Vanderbilt, Roy Kramer, was great about it. So was Evelyn, even though she knew it would require a real commitment on my part. She always has been good about supporting me on things she knew I really wanted to do.

Although Bob and I are very different temperamentally, we had developed a mutual respect. From the first time I met him, I was very straight up with him and he likes that. That's how he operates best. He just has to feel comfortable with you. He's also one of the few totally honest people you'll ever meet, almost to a fault. Say, for example, that you've got a wart on your nose. Most people wouldn't say anything about it or they'd try to bring it to your attention in a tactful way. But Bob would say, "What the hell are you doing with a wart on your nose?" Whether you're a player or a coach, you always know where you stand with him.

I thought he was way ahead of his time as a teacher of basketball and, although he has gotten a lot of attention for his intense man-to-man defense, I thought he was much more innovative offensively, with the way he used screens and cuts. He's very much a purist and I am, too. We have a lot in common when it comes to the way we feel about how the game should be played, the value we place on history and tradition, and the importance of academics. Yet we have enough mutual respect that we also can disagree with each other. I'm sure there are some things from a discipline standpoint that I would do differently than he would. It's sort of like painting a house. You can roll it, brush it or spray it. But if the house comes out looking pretty, it doesn't make any difference how you did it.

By the time the Olympic tryouts began in April 1984, Bob's two-year plan was working very well. He had sent Raveling and Donoher around the world to scout teams. He himself had scouted the Russians, even though they had said they were going to boycott the Los Angeles Games in retaliation for our 1980 boycott of their games. He built a tape library of our possible opponents, as well as the American players who would be trying out for the 14 spots (12 regulars and two alternates) on our team. At first, we thought we would keep the tryouts small, inviting only 36 or 42 players to come to Bloomington. But Bob kept saying, "Let's not overlook anybody." By the time the tryouts began, we had 73 players to evaluate.

It was a wonderful experience, a little like basketball heaven. The level of play was really high, and all the players got a really good look not only from our staff, but from the other coaches who Bob brought in to advise us. Former Olympic coaches Pete Newell, Dean Smith, Dave Gavitt and Henry Iba were there. So were Mike Krzyzewski, Clarence "Big House" Gaines, Digger Phelps and others. Every day we would meet at some place like Smitty's, one of Bob's favorite spots, for lunch, then we would meet and have dinner again at night. From day one, Bob said, "We're not selecting an all-star group, we're selecting a basketball team." That meant that we were to concern ourselves with identifying the players who were unselfish and who could fill roles.

During those initial tryouts, Charles Barkley, then at Auburn, was probably the most dominant player. When we finally trimmed the group down to the 18 we invited back for a mini-camp, Charles showed up badly out of shape. It was obvious to all of us that he hadn't been serious about being ready to play. But when he didn't make the team and some lesser-talented players did, Charles made some derogatory comments and the media picked up on it. How could we pick a Jon Koncak or a Joe Kleine instead of Charles? The reason was that accepting roles was a critical part of it. Charles could have made the team, but he demonstrated his lack of commitment by not reporting to the mini-camp in reasonable playing condition.

Bob had said from the beginning that he wanted big guards. So we picked Jordan, Alvin Robertson of Arkansas, Vern Fleming of Georgia, Steve Alford of Indiana and Leon Wood of Cal State Fullerton. He also wanted flexibility, guys who could play more than one position. Jordan certainly fit that criterion. So did Sam Perkins of North Carolina, Wayman Tisdale of Oklahoma, Chris Mullin of St. John's and Jeff Turner, who had played so well for me at Vanderbilt. At the time we picked the team, Bob still believed that we would have to play the Russians and, therefore, would need some big bodies. So we picked Kleine of Arkansas and Koncak of SMU to back up Georgetown's Patrick Ewing at center. Our alternates were Chuck Person of Auburn and Johnny Dawkins of Duke.

The selections of Alford, who had completed his freshman year at Indiana, and Turner meant that Bob and I were subjected to charges of nepotism. But the truth is, the rest of the staff had to convince Bob to take Alford. We looked at our team and saw that Mullin was our only zone-buster, so we needed Alford because of his shooting ability and his range. As for Turner, he kind of just played his way onto the team. I stayed out of it. But he could play three positions and he was just a great person who would be a good team player. As it turned out, both Steve and Jeff made significant contributions in Los Angeles.

When we began practicing in Bloomington, Bob explained to the players what the expectations were, and he emphasized it by placing a photo of a gold medal in everybody's locker. Although we emphasized unselfishness and team play, it was obvious from day one that Michael Jordan would be the star of our team. When I had taken him to Europe a couple of years earlier, he scored a lot of points, but he was still young and inexperienced. It was interesting to me to see how much he had matured. I remember Bob saying, "I've never coached a player like this before, who can do all the things he can do." Besides that, Michael was a tremendous competitor. He wanted to win at anything he did. There wasn't much to do in Bloomington, so the coaches decided to practice early so we could play golf in the afternoon. Steve Alford and another Indiana player, Dan Dakich, began taking Michael out to play golf and he just fell in love with it. But, typically, he wasn't content just to be playing. He wanted to play well.

Thanks largely to the efforts of the folks at ABAUSA, particularly executive director Bill Wall and associate Tom McGrath, we were able to do some things that previous Olympic staffs hadn't been able to do. In particular, there was a series of exhibition games that prepared our team to play against anybody. After an exhibition in Bloomington against former Indiana players, we played an NBA All-Star team in Indianapolis. Their team included Larry Bird, Magic Johnson, Isiah Thomas and Mark Aguirre. It was the first big basketball event that had been held in the Hoosier Dome and it was nationally televised. It was just a tremendous thing for international basketball in our country.

All told, we played nine exhibitions around the country against NBA players and we won them all. When we were on the road, Bob and I got away from basketball by playing tennis. He beat me some early on, but then I caught on to his game and turned the tables on him. I remember one game in Minneapolis where I was serving on match point. He hit his return and knew right away that it was long, so he just let go of the racket. I yelled, "The ball's out, but the racket's in!" Like Michael, Bob wants to win at anything he does.

Before we arrived in Los Angeles, we had our final camp in San Diego. We were ready to go, but these were the dog days for us. How hard do you practice at this point? We were lucky in that the NBA had a rookie league going. That was good because it gave us different people to scrimmage against. Bob also brought in some interesting speakers to address the team. The list included older basketball coaches such as Pete Newell, Mr. Iba and Everett Dean, but Bob also brought in Bill Bradley, the former star player with Princeton and the New York Knicks who was then a U.S. Senator from New Jersey, and Johnny Bench, the former great catcher with the Cincinnati Reds.

We ate out every night. It was an eating marathon. I must have gained 20 pounds. Bench was there most of the time, and every time we went out, he and Bob would be asked for autographs. Bob tried to deflect it somewhat by introducing the rest of us. "This is Coach Iba," he would say, "or this is Coach Newton." But Bob and Bench were the celebrities everyone recognized. One night I got to the restaurant early and worked out a deal with a waitress. She came up to our table and said, "Coach, I've admired you and respected you ... would you please sign this for me?" Bob reached for her piece of paper, as I knew he would, and then she said, "Yes, Coach Newton, I've always admired you." I said, "Oh, sure, where are you from ... You probably would like to get Coach Knight's autograph, too."

Well, it was priceless. Bob looked confused. Pete Newell and Bench got a big laugh out of it. You don't get the chance to put one over on Bob very often, but that was one time where I got him.

We made the decision in San Diego that we would go by bus to Los Angeles and go through the security process as any other country would. We would have a press conference at the same time we went through the checks, then go on to the Olympic Village, which, in our case, was a high-rise dorm at Southern Cal. But right before we left San Diego, Bill Wall came to me and said, "You've got to talk to Coach Knight because he says he's not going to do the press conference." It seems that one of the Los Angeles papers had printed a really biting article about Bob, and he had decided he just didn't want to mess around with the media. So I went to him and said, "You've already convinced everybody in the U.S. press that you're not going to have anything to do with them, but now you've got the world press to deal with. Do you think you should deprive them of your wit and your charm?" I laid it on pretty thick. Finally he said, "Charles, we're going to do the press conference." He always called me Charles when he was in a good mood.

At the opening ceremonies, I was the only member of our basketball staff who walked into the Los Angeles Coliseum with the American team. As the host country, we were the last ones to be introduced. I'll just never forget what a thrill it was. A band played "The Stars and Stripes Forever," and the crowd never stopped roaring as we walked around the track. It was a happening, the way the athletes from around the world interacted and I'll always be grateful that I participated.

As far as our living quarters were concerned, Bob, Raveling and I were supposed to share a room in one of the high-rise dorms at USC. George got there early and had all his stuff laid out. When Bob and I came in, we noticed right away that the air-conditioning didn't work. I called the Olympic people in the office and told them we couldn't sleep there. They said it was too late to fix the air-conditioning, but that we could stay temporarily in a suite on a higher floor. It was being reserved for our yachting team and they hadn't arrived yet.

So Bob and I go up there, but George decides to stay put. It was a suite, sure enough, with a kitchenette, a living-room area and double-bunks in the bedrooms. I called the Olympic people back and said, "Is there any way we can keep this for awhile? Can we use this until the yachting people show up?" Well, we stayed one night. And then another. And then another. We've got our soft drinks in the refrigerator and Bob has set up our video equipment. After four or five days, we were really getting used to it. Then one night we're out in the Olympic Village and Bob sees a guy that has a bag with "U.S. Yachting Team" on the side. We figured the yachting team had finally arrived and we would have to move back in with George. I thought Bob was going to cry. But it turned out that the guy was there to tell the Olympic people that the yachting team wasn't coming, that it had decided to stay elsewhere. Needless to say, we were tickled.

One other thing I remember is that there was a fire station right outside the gate in the Olympic Village at USC. The firemen had a little basketball court out back. One night, as we were walking back to the dorm, the firemen recognized Bob and said, "Hey, Coach Knight, come in here and we'll show you where we play." And that's how the firemen became a part of our team. From then on, we had a lot of our pregame walk-throughs at the fire station court.

Living in the Olympic Village was a great experience for the players and the coaches. Evelyn stayed at the Marriott by the airport with Carol George, her former college roommate and best friend, and I would hook up with her on our days off. She went to all the diving events. Other than basketball, that was about all I got to see. But in the Olympic Village, they had an all-night buffet and you got to interact with our athletes from other sports and athletes from other countries. Because of my connection to the SEC, I spent some time with Harvey Glance, the sprinter, and Rowdy Gaines, the swimmer. I also developed a sweet tooth. Snickers was one of the corporate sponsors, and there were literally mounds of them in the dining room. I got to the point where I had to grab a couple of Snickers bars every night.

As team manager, I was basically our athletics director. I would go out and meet with the local organizing committee to set up our arrangements in the Village. I toured the Forum with Gail Goodrich, the former UCLA and pro basketball star who was our liaison with the organizing committee. I made the arrangements for our video equipment and did a lot of general administrative duties, such as attending the drug-testing meetings. The team manager was the only one accredited to get into the drug-testing area. Late in a game, I'd go to the game manager and draw balls out of a box to see which of our players would be tested. It was a lot of work, but I was lucky to have access to ABAUSA staff.

We won our first five games by an average of 39 points to advance to the medal round, but Bob still got a little edgy. We hadn't played particularly well in beating West Germany, so after practice the next day Bob and I stopped by a Baskin-Robbins to get some ice cream. We've got our USA coaching garb on, so we're easily recognizable. Bob was telling me about how he was tired and how all the hype was wearing him down when a kid standing in line said, "Hey, that's Coach Knight." An older woman also in line said, "Who's Coach Knight?" When the youngster said he was our Olympic basketball coach, the woman said, "What's the Olympics?" As a way of trying to get Bob to relax, I used that to tell him that there were millions of people who couldn't care less if we won or lost, or even if the Games were held. He didn't buy it.

One of the humorous sidelights was the rapport that Bob struck up with a French interpreter. It started after our first game, when Bob questioned one of her translations. She fired right back at him and he liked that. From then on, his give-and-take with the interpreter was more entertaining than most of our games. After we defeated Spain, 96-65, to win the gold medal, she gave Bob a little stuffed animal and he presented her with a bottle of California wine.

In the first half of the final game, referee Nars Zanlin, a Canadian, called goaltending against Ewing. Bob exploded and was called for his first technical foul of the Olympics. Part of this was because many of the officials didn't seem to understand English. If Bob would get on them, they would just look puzzled. Bob was so angry at Zanlin that he said, "I may get into this guy again." I told him not to do it because Zanlin understood English and, in international basketball, you were ejected after two technicals. "Charles," he said, "Are you sure? Only two?" I assured him that if he got another technical, he would be the first coach in Olympic history to be in the locker room when his team won the gold medal.

Shortly after that technical, we went on a tear in which we expanded a six-point lead to 23 late in the first half. From then on, it was simply a matter of waiting for the game to end and the celebration to begin. Except for Bob, that is. He jerked Tisdale out of the game in the second half and chewed him out, even though we had a 68-48 lead at the time. In the last few seconds, Bob leaned over to me and said, "Charles, I don't know where you're going to be four years from now, but I'm going to be fishing or doing anything except coaching one of these basketball teams." I know what he meant. We all felt exhilarated, but drained.

After the game, the players cut down the nets, put one of them around Bob's neck, and carried him around the floor. But Bob had another plan. He insisted that the team get Mr. Iba, who had been the coach when our 1972 Olympic team lost to the Russians in Munich, and give him a victory ride. This was the side of Bob that few people ever see. Mr. Iba had just lost his wife, and Bob saw to it that he was involved with our team. The fact that he brought Mr. Iba along through the entire process and kept him involved probably prolonged his life. I don't know of any other coach who would have been that thoughtful, but Bob, who loves to talk about basketball tradition and history, always really cared about older coaches such as Mr. Iba, Nat Holman, Clair Bee and Joe Lapchick.

This was to be the last time the U.S. won the gold medal

with an amateur team. Our team was fun to watch because Bob had our players so prepared that it was downright scary. It was Michael Jordan's international coming-out party, but he was hardly a one-man show. Immediately the media tried to compare our team with the 1960 U.S. gold-medal team that included Oscar Robertson and Jerry West. That's a good debate, but I'll say this on behalf of our team: I don't think anybody ever played as hard, as smart and as well together for as long a time as this team did. You also have to consider that the rest of world was a lot better in 1984 than it was in 1960. And, finally, we had in Michael Jordan a superstar who would eventually be recognized as the greatest who ever played the game.

The staff didn't get gold medals. But Bob had some made up and mailed one to each of us. It's still one of my most treasured possessions.

Chapter 7
As Coach Bryant Said, You've Got to Listen When Mama Calls

I 've always liked country music, and one of the positive things about being the Vanderbilt basketball coach is that a lot of the stars like sports. So that worked out great for me. Evelyn and I could go hear music anytime we wanted, and a lot of the entertainers would come to our games. We got to know the Oak Ridge Boys, Boots Randolph, Floyd Kramer, Dicky Lee, Barbara Mandrell, Vince Gill, Brenda Lee, Conway Twitty, the Gatlin Brothers and many more. Right after Christmas, we would have our Music City Invitational Tournament, and usually somebody from the country music world was our honorary chairman. However, when I went into the 1984-85 season, I knew I had better start producing some winning teams or somebody might have to write a sad country song about me.

Roy Kramer, the athletics director when I coached at Vanderbilt, was great about my participation with the 1984 Olympic team. I had received some criticism from fans who thought I should have spent that summer in Nashville, considering the transitional state of our basket-ball program. But Roy understood the positive side of my involvement. When you go into a recruit's home and can talk about coaching Michael Jordan at the Olympics, that's something that will get their attention. I felt our program was going to be okay. We just needed to keep plugging and do a better job of recruiting. I had gone back to my philosophy of identifying late-bloomers instead of trying to recruit the nation's top 100 prospects. So we brought in players such as Barry Goheen, Scott Draud, Frank Kornet, Brett Burrow and Barry Booker. They were young-sters who fit our profile, and they turned out to be won-derful players for us.

With Booker, for example, it came down to us and Tennessee. But by the time Tennessee got involved, we were okay. Barry was the youngest of 11 children, and all of them turned out to be successful college graduates. His parents ran a family-oriented filling station in Franklin, Tenn. If you were going to describe an absolutely func-tional family, the Bookers would be it. When I made my visit, seven of the siblings sat in on it, and nobody has ever asked me questions about a program the way they did. For me, it was a fascinating experience. I really enjoyed it. Barry now is an analyst for CBS. He's very good at it too, which doesn't surprise me in the least.

Goheen also turned out to be a great player for us. At the end of the game, he wanted the ball and we wanted to get it to him. I would say, "Let's just Goheen 'em." One of the funniest things that ever happened to me as a coach involved Goheen. We were playing Georgia. They got a man open, but Frank Kornet blocked his shot. Now we're two points down, with less than 15 seconds to play, and Booker comes out on the break with the ball. He passes to Goheen, who was open for a mid-range jumper. But instead, he dribbled the ball to the corner and shot a three. I thought, "My God, he doesn't know the score." We just had used a timeout and we talked about taking it into overtime. But at the horn Goheen throws up this three-pointer. It goes in and we win by a point. I went directly to Barry and before I could ask him if he knew the score he said, "I knew the score, but I didn't think your heart could take an overtime." He was probably right.

When the NCAA rules committee approved the three-point shot before the 1986-87 season, we really took advantage of it. I had chaired the rules committee, so I knew the value of it. Some coaches, not to mention any names, were real stubborn about it because it essentially eliminated the mid-range jump shot. From then on, the game was going to be about dunks and three-pointers. I felt that the spacing between players on offense would be important, so we worked on that. The result was we led

157

the league in three-pointers. The new rule forced us to recognize the guy who could shoot off the perimeter. It really helped us, and we took advantage of it. So after going 11-17 in 1984-85 and 13-15 the next year, we turned it around. In 1986-87, we earned a spot in the NIT with a final record of 18-16.

One of the most important players I ever recruited was Will Perdue, a 7-footer who epitomized my recruiting philosophy. As a high school player from Merritt Island, Fla., Will was very difficult to evaluate. He never played against anybody his size, so he had it pretty easy. But when I saw him at a camp in Milledgeville, Ga., I became convinced that he had what it took. Playing against competition his own size, some of whom were better athletes, he showed heart, desire, good skills and the ability to run the floor. I left that camp knowing he would be the one big, young guy we needed to recruit. So much of recruiting is just instinct and luck.

I always had a rule that in order to play, you had to be on schedule to graduate. I had it at Transylvania, I had it at Alabama and I had it at Vanderbilt. If it took summer school to get on track, that was fine with me. But Will fell off schedule during his freshman year. He had chosen engineering as his major, not because he liked it, but because that was his dad's choice. So we reached a point where he was eligible by NCAA rules, but not by my rule.

His dad was very upset, and Will started talking about transferring. I was in a real pickle because I didn't want to lose him, but I also didn't want to make an exception to what I thought was a very strong rule.

I scheduled a meeting with him and I stayed up much of the night, making notes on my legal pad. When he came in, I gave him about 15 minutes of my best arguments. When I was done, I was certain he was going to leave. He said he would let me know. When he finally said he was going to stay, we gave him a redshirt year to take the pressure off and allow him to get his act together academically. That was one of the best things that ever happened to Will. As a junior and senior, he led us in scoring, rebounding and blocked shots. In his senior year, 1987-88, we earned a spot in the NCAA Tournament and won two games before losing to Kansas, the eventual NCAA champion. Our final record that season was 20-11, the school's first 20-win season since 1974. I was named the SEC Coach of the Year that season and Will was named SEC Athlete of the Year, but a lot of credit belonged to John Bostick and Ed Martin. Much like Harry Lancaster had worked with Bill Spivey years earlier when I was a Kentucky player, John and Ed had worked with Perdue on his footwork and technique.

I remember a couple of funny things about Will after we lost to Kansas. The first was that whenever we rode a team bus, I always sat in the right front seat. I didn't get there early, but I was always on time. I would say to our trainer, Joe Worden, "Is everybody here?" Well, many times Evelyn wasn't there. She was timely, but not necessarily on time. I would absent-mindedly say, "Where in the hell is Evelyn?" So the day after we lose to Kansas, Will is sitting in my seat. I walk with Evelyn right on past him. Then I heard him say, "Joe, is that everybody? Where in the hell is Evelyn?" The guys on the team cracked up.

Then I had a talk with Will about his redshirt year. I asked him, "Remember the day when you came into my office and I thought you were going to leave? What really changed your mind?" I thought he would say it was that 15-minute power talk I gave him. But he told me he went back to his dorm, met some buddies and went to a local pub. After a beer or two his buddies said, "Will, you don't want to leave us." He agreed with them and decided to stay. As he told me, "I was ready to tell you I was coming back, but then you got all wound up so I let you go on." Regardless, it was great that he stayed. After playing so well for us, he went on to a long NBA career and even got some championship rings as a valuable member of Michael Jordan's Chicago Bulls.

So we had it going pretty good heading into the 1988-89 season. We had some good young players and had answered all the questions about whether we could get it done at Vanderbilt without sacrificing academics. But I was at a point where I was beginning to think about older coaches who had stayed too long at the dance and ended up with a lot of bad players late in their career. That has the makings of a country song, doesn't it? When I went out recruiting, the first question often asked was, "Do you intend to be there all four years of my son's career?" That had to come from rivals. It wasn't so much that they were planting bad things about you, but they were floating the idea that you might not be around much longer. I didn't want this to happen to me personally and I didn't want it to happen to Vanderbilt. Still, when I went into the 1988-89 season, I didn't know it would be my final one as a coach.

In December, I got a call from Dr. David Roselle, the president at Kentucky, and I was almost rude to him. He said he was looking for somebody to replace Cliff Hagan as his athletics director. I told him I wasn't interested. I told him that Cliff was a former teammate of mine and had done a good job at Kentucky in many ways. "In my opinion," I said, "you're getting rid of the wrong person." But Dr. Roselle was persistent. He said he would like to have a talk with me about the whole situation at Kentucky. I told John Bibb, the veteran columnist of *The Tennessean* in Nashville, that I had no interest in going to Kentucky and that my only goal was coaching the Vanderbilt basketball team. I wasn't lying. That's really the way I felt at the time.

So that was it until Dr. Roselle called me back and asked

me to meet him in Elizabethtown, Ky. He said, "I'd like to explain what's happened here, and I really need some help in picking the right guy to replace Cliff." I told Evelyn I needed to talk to him because, after all, it was my alma mater. So we met on a Sunday in the president's office of Elizabethtown Community College. After about three hours, Dr. Roselle convinced me that he not only wanted me, but that I was needed. The need part got to me. Whenever Coach Bryant was asked why he left Texas A&M to take the Alabama job, he always said, "Mama called." When you feel your alma mater needs you, it's a powerful tug. After our meeting in Elizabethtown, I had another meeting in Bowling Green with Dr. Charles Wethington, who was chairing the search committee. In early January, they called and offered me the job.

At that point in my life, it was a challenge that was very exciting. The Kentucky basketball program was a mess because of various highly publicized problems. In Los Angeles, an Emery air freight envelope from the UK basketball office to recruit Chris Mills had broken open, revealing $1,000. There were charges of academic fraud involving a player named Eric Manuel. And some other things. Eddie Sutton, who had replaced Joe Hall as the Kentucky coach in 1985, was fighting to save his job. There was a mess to clean up, but in Dr. Roselle there also was a president who wanted to get it cleaned up, who was willing to take the heat and who would give me the tools I needed to succeed.

I told Dr. Roselle and Dr. Wethington that I would take the job only with the understanding that I would have vice-presidential status, but not the title. In other words, I would be, in effect, the university's vice-president in charge of athletics. That meant that I would report directly to Dr. Roselle and have the freedom to recommend coaches to him. To restructure the program, I really needed that freedom and flexibility. I also wanted to bring John Bostick with me to be in charge of compliance if he didn't get the Vanderbilt job. So this thing kind of grabbed me. When I talked with Evelyn, however, she balked for the second time in our married life. The first was when we left Transylvania for Alabama. Now she didn't want to leave Nashville. "You told me this (going to Vanderbilt) would be our last move," she reminded me. "We're both happy here, we're nestled in pretty good, and you've got the program going after some lean years. Now here you are, almost 60, and wanting to move again?" She was rather adamant about it. "If you take this job," she said, "maybe we can meet in Bowling Green on weekends." But, bless her, she finally came around.

I had kept Roy Kramer in the loop on the thing and we announced it in late January. It was something that you couldn't, and shouldn't, keep quiet. Most of the Vanderbilt people were great, but John Bibb really drilled me in *The*

Tennessean. He said that I had lied to him and should leave right away because I was a lame-duck coach. But as I told our players, "I may be lame and I may be a duck, but I'm not a lame duck, so don't test me." On Feb. 8, 1989, Kentucky came into our place and we beat them, 81-51. The press box at Vanderbilt is near the ceiling and, after that game, John leaned out and waved a white towel at me. He was surrendering. I had to laugh.

My last game as a coach was an 81-65 loss to Notre Dame in the first round of the NCAA Tournament on March 17, 1989. With Booker, Goheen and Kornet as our tri-captains, our final record was 19-14. I was going to have some good players coming back the next season and you always hate to leave talent. I thought Roy Kramer made a mistake in not naming John Bostick to replace me, but at least that enabled me to bring John to Kentucky to be in charge of compliance. Eddie Fogler, who succeeded me, had a 21-14 record in his first season. So it was the same situation as at Alabama, which I also had left in good shape. It was difficult to leave coaching, but I felt that, just as I had proved I could contribute as a player at Kentucky, so had I proved that I could coach with anybody. The only thing I didn't do was coach a national championship team. I also had paid my dues by working with USA Basketball, the National Association of Basketball Coaches and the NCAA Rules Committee. I felt pretty good about all that.

On April 1, 1989, I officially came on board at Kentucky. My intent was to give them seven good years. That would enable me to fulfill my duties with USA Basketball and go through the 1996 Olympics. The biggest thing I gave up in coming back to Kentucky was income. I was making about $400,000 a year at Vanderbilt and I became the Kentucky athletics director for around $110,000 a year. But money wasn't a significant issue for me. I had saved some dollars at Vanderbilt, and Kentucky gave me an annuity where I'd make up some of the money if I fulfilled my contract.

I was just honored that Dr. Roselle thought I could do the job and, as I said earlier, I felt there was a real need. Of course, there also was risk. I could have stayed at Vanderbilt with a relative degree of comfort for the rest of my career. I had enjoyed a pretty good coaching career and a measure of national stature. I told Evelyn that we could go to Lexington and everything could backfire. With the problems they had at the time, I could fall right on my fanny. But I remembered some of the things I had learned growing up, about how my folks let me have the freedom to be on my own and about how sometimes you need to take risks.

But I'll tell you this: Had I known that Jerry Claiborne was going to retire as the Kentucky football coach, I might have done some serious rethinking.

Chapter 8
Well, They Didn't Promise Me a Rose Garden

T he Lexington to which I returned in 1989 was a far different city from the one I knew as a University of Kentucky student-athlete and the coach at Transylvania. When I made the decision to come, my daughter Tracy came with me. We walked from the Campbell House Inn to the campus, and my first reaction was just about how big the university had become. The enrollment probably was around 7,500 when I was a student. I reminisced a lot, showed Tracy where my history class was, things like that. Having made the decision, I was really excited about getting back, although I knew it wasn't going to be an easy job.

A lot of people feel that when you go into a new job, you've got to make big changes. My feeling is that you've got to bring your chiefs with you — for example, I hired John Bostick as the first full-time compliance administrator anywhere — but that there's also great value keeping people who were doing a good job. So I opted to keep Larry Ivy,

Gene DeFilippo and many of the people who were here under Cliff Hagan, and they turned out to be as good as I thought they were. In dealing with the staff, I've found it's better to make changes slowly. Plus, it's the fair thing to do.

Past that, my No. 1 challenge as Kentucky's athletics director was to deal with the embarrassment and anger over whatever it was that happened in Eddie Sutton's basketball program. Unfortunately for Eddie, he had decided to get into a power struggle with Dr. Roselle during his last months on the job, and coaches never win those things. As a result, there was a huge residue of misinformation and hostility that had to be overcome. Everybody seemed angry with somebody. Some were pointing fingers at the NCAA. They felt UK was being picked on. With others, it was Dr. Roselle and Judge Jim Park, who had conducted the university's in-house investigation. This element felt the university should have stonewalled the NCAA instead of cooperating with it. Others were angry with the media, Eddie and so forth.

So my first task was to get out into the state and start mending fences. In my first 18 days on the job, I went to 21 different areas of the state. I spoke to alumni groups, civic clubs, whoever wanted me. My message was always the same: We're screwed up right now, but we've got a president who wants to do it right and hire the right person as our basketball coach. I emphasized that we wanted to compete for national championships, but that we also would stress compliance and academics. I was pleased to learn that the people out in the state were very receptive to what I said and supportive of the university.

As I told Dr. Roselle when I was hired, the single most important decision that I would make as athletics director would be the hiring of Coach Sutton's replacement. I felt that if we didn't hire the right guy, we could go the way of UCLA, which went into a deep decline after Coach John Wooden's retirement in 1975. With that in mind, I began the search by calling four or five basketball people whom I really respect. People such as Bob Knight of Indiana; Tom Butters, then the athletics director at Duke; and Roy Kramer, my former boss at Vanderbilt. When I called Dave Gavitt at Providence, he said, "You've got to talk to Rick Pitino ... I've heard that he's not really happy with the Knicks, even though they're doing well." I tucked that away.

My original short list included such proven winners as Mike Krzyzewski, Pat Riley, Lute Olson, Terry Holland, Lee Rose and Pat Summitt. Yes, that's the same Pat Summitt, a female, who has won umpteen women's titles at Tennessee. When I mentioned that to Evelyn, she said, "Great, C.M., do it!" I was serious. I think Pat's good enough to coach anywhere. But I began by going through the other names on my list. Some said, right off the bat, that they weren't interested because they didn't think it was a good job. Why would they leave their current jobs to come into a program that was in such disarray? I personally eliminated Lee Rose, my former player and assistant at Transylvania, because I just felt he wasn't the person who could rally the support we needed. That created a rift between us, and I hated that because Lee always will be an important part of my life. But my sole obligation was to do what I thought was best for the University of Kentucky.

I finally got it down to P.J. Carlesimo, who had just taken Seton Hall to the NCAA championship game, and Lute, who had developed Final Four teams at Iowa and Arizona. I was convinced they could do the job the way I wanted it done. It was sort of like recruiting players — I only wanted individuals who wanted us. I wasn't interested in anybody who just wanted the money. So I said to both of them, "If I offered you this job, would you take it?" I didn't think it would be in the university's best interest at that time to risk offering the job outright and be turned down. The media was on my doorstep from day one, and that was something I had to be concerned about.

Fortunately, I also had gotten permission from Al Bianchi, then the general manager of the Knicks, to talk to Rick Pitino. I really admired the way Rick had coached his teams at Providence (he went to the 1987 Final Four by beating a great Alabama team in the regional) and with the Knicks. During our first conversation, he said, "The decision is, the pros or college?" He said Kentucky was the only college program he would consider. In that clever way of his, he told me Kentucky was the "Roman empire of college basketball." At the same time, however, the Knicks were going to the playoffs and he was committed to that. He said, "I'm not your candidate ... I'm out of it." He recommended that I hire P.J. But at that time I didn't think either P.J. or Lute was going to accept the challenge.

Something in my gut just told me to wait until his season was over, so I just decided we would wait and see what happened to the Knicks in the playoffs. As soon as they were defeated, I called Rick and said, "Would you just sit down and talk with me?" We met at the Westchester, N.Y., airport. He arrived in a Mercedes sports coupe. It was our first serious one-on-one meeting, and I was immediately impressed with his charm. He invited me to come to his home. He lived in a neighborhood with big houses that reminded me of Tara in the movie, "Gone with the Wind." I met Joanne, his wife, and it couldn't have been nicer. I was as up front with him as I could be. "We want you to coach at Kentucky," I said, "but we've got some problems." I told him we would construct a long-term contract where the first two years would be throw-away years. I told him our people were not used to losing and that the expectations would be huge. I recruited him just as I would a player, telling him about the beauty marks and the warts. When I asked him to come visit and take a look, he agreed.

Rick came in only a week or so after the NCAA announced the sanctions against the Kentucky program — no postseason play for two years, a reduction in scholarships, four years probation. When we were having dinner at the Coach House, a reporter from the *Lexington Herald-Leader* wanted to ask Rick about being charged with NCAA violations 15 years earlier when he was a young assistant at Hawaii. When that got out, some of our fans accused the paper of trying to sabotage the efforts to hire Rick.

There was such enormous interest that we held a press conference for Rick. One of the things he said was, "I think the University of Kentucky will get turned around in a very short time with me as coach." He also said we shouldn't offer him the job "if there's a shadow of a doubt about Rick Pitino," but added that "There's no one in this business with more character than Rick Pitino." Asked about Hawaii, Rick said, "I didn't make any mistakes at Hawaii" and that the NCAA investigation had "exonerated" him. I agreed and so did Dr. Roselle.

Although Rick and I are different in personality and temperament, we have some things in common. He's a purist, a traditionalist, and so am I. He really enjoys a challenge, and so do I. So I think I really got Rick's competitive juices flowing. When he finally decided to take the job, it was the best thing that ever happened to the

Kentucky program. With the disarray we were in, he was the best fit. He wanted the job and understood what needed to be done. He had the toughness for it. And, finally, he was way ahead of his time as a coach. It was kind of like Wendell Hudson and Leon Douglas and Charles Cleveland coming to Alabama. Just as they made me a good coach, so did the hiring of Rick make me a good athletics director. I'll always be grateful to Rick and Joanne for their willingness to take a risk. And I just knew he would get our basketball program back to where it should be. At the press conference where Rick's hiring was announced, he mentioned a *Sports Illustrated* cover story, "Kentucky's Shame," that detailed our problems. "Someday we're going to be back on the *SI* cover," said Rick, "and it's going to be for winning the NCAA championship."

After hiring Rick, I turned my energies to football — specifically, raising the money for the fieldhouse we needed to complement Commonwealth Stadium. Under Jerry Claiborne, who had played for Coach Bryant at Kentucky and coached under him at Alabama, we were bopping along reasonably well, playing everybody on our schedule tough. A proven winner during his head coaching career at Virginia Tech and Maryland, Jerry was my kind of coach in that he wouldn't think of cheating and he stressed academics. When he replaced Fran Curci after the 1981 season, Jerry inherited a program that had a lot of problems in the areas of compliance, discipline and academics. The price he paid was an 0-10-1 record his first season. After that, however, he went 41-36-2 and produced two bowl teams. Besides that, his teams ranked among the SEC leaders in academics. As far as I was concerned, Jerry could be the Kentucky football coach as long as he wanted.

But during the 1989 season he told me, "I need to talk to you right after the season." After we finished a tough 6-5 with a 31-10 loss to Tennessee on Nov. 25 in Commonwealth, Jerry came to me and said, "Faye (his wife) and I have decided that it's time for me to retire." That came as a shock to me and everybody else. It just ruined my Thanksgiving. All he asked was that we keep his staff on contract until they could find another job, which we did. But I respected Jerry's integrity so much that I asked him to stay on and help me raise funds for the fieldhouse, which he agreed to do.

So I did the same thing I did with the basketball job. I began calling football people whom I respected and began making a list of candidates. I wanted somebody who would continue the academic and compliance tradition that Jerry had started, who had a good football pedigree, and who was a proven winner. At the top of my list was Bill Curry, who then was in the process of taking Alabama to the Sugar Bowl. I had known and admired Bill for years, so I called his agent, Robert Fraley of Orlando, Fla., to see if it was true that Bill was unhappy with Alabama. He had never been accepted in Tuscaloosa for various reasons. Not playing for Coach Bryant was one of them. But worse than that, in the eyes of many hardcore Alabama fans, was that he had played and coached at Georgia Tech. Coach Bryant had a long-standing feud with former Tech coach Bobby Dodd. In Alabama, they carry grudges a long time.

When Bill told Fraley to tell me he wasn't interested, it didn't take me long to identify Mike Shanahan, then an assistant with the Denver Broncos, as being the football equivalent of Rick Pitino. I offered him the job and, when he left Lexington to go back to Denver, I was sure he was going to take it. But the Broncos wanted to keep him so badly that they made him a counter-offer that he couldn't refuse. Like Rick, the choice with Mike came down to whether he wanted to be in college or the pros. He stuck with the NFL, and was eventually rewarded when, as the Broncos' head coach, he won back-to-back Super Bowls in 1997 and 1998.

While I was recruiting Shanahan in early December, Alabama athletics director Hootie Ingram, whom I had worked with during my days in the SEC office, presented Curry with a new contract offer that Bill considered insulting. It stripped him of much of his authority — the right to hire and fire assistants, for example — and gave the university the right to fire him, at any time, without cause or compensation for outside income. When I heard about this in late December, I called Fraley again. When Curry told Fraley he might be interested, I called Hootie to get permission to meet with Bill. On Saturday, Dec. 30, 1989, I flew to New Orleans, where Bill was getting his team ready to play Miami in the Sugar Bowl, and met with him for about 15 minutes the next day in his hotel room.

He was so focused on the game that I left the room thinking I had made a mistake. I really didn't feel good about it, although I did feel he was interested. He told me that he and Carolyn (Curry's wife) were not going to do anything at all until after the Sugar Bowl. They were going to drive back to Tuscaloosa from New Orleans and use that five hours to talk about the future. He promised me that he would not lead us on.

On the afternoon of Tuesday, Jan. 2, Bill called me to say he wanted to come the next day for a visit. When that news broke in Alabama, all heck broke loose. Many Crimson Tide supporters were upset and embarrassed that their coach would even consider leaving for a program that had consistently finished in the SEC's second division. After our meeting in Lexington, Bill and Carolyn went back to Tuscaloosa to think. By this time they were receiving flowers and telegrams from fans who wanted them to stay. Heck, Carolyn even received a diamond-encrusted elephant (the Alabama mascot) from Coach

Bryant's granddaughter, Mary Harmon Moman.

On Saturday, Jan. 6, I called Bill during the Kentucky-Vanderbilt basketball game to say that since Evelyn and I were already in Nashville, we might as well go on to Tuscaloosa the next day. When Bill told me to come ahead, I felt really good. The next day, over some homemade chicken salad, Bill and Carolyn told us that they were coming to Kentucky. Later that day, Bill broke the news to his Alabama players. He then took a private plane to Lexington, where our athletics board ratified his appointment. Bill told the media he made the decision for the same reason I left Vanderbilt — he felt wanted and needed.

The only potential problem was that Dr. Roselle was leaving. He was the perfect president for me, a man with a brilliant intellect to go with a lot of good ol' common sense. He had a vision of the way things should be in our athletics program and the toughness to back it up. I don't really think he left because of his controversial role in the basketball scandal. He was simply concerned that funding for higher education in Kentucky was going the wrong way, and here was Delaware, offering him a great deal. I didn't like it that the man who hired me was leaving, but I still felt comfortable with my role. I had to assure Bill that, at age 59, I planned to stay on the job at least until I reached retirement age. I also assured him that the new president wouldn't undermine my authority in athletics.

Fortunately for us, the university named Dr. Charles Wethington to replace Dr. Roselle. From then until now, he has been the best possible president to work for. He has a great understanding of how athletics fits into the mission of the university, and he was totally supportive of our efforts. His stature in intercollegiate athletics grew to the point where he was named chairman of the executive committee of the NCAA.

Right after we hired Bill, I talked with someone who mentioned the "Big Four" in an athletics director's career: hiring a basketball coach, hiring a football coach, dealing with NCAA probation and changing presidents. "That's an A.D.'s career," this person said. "Heck," I answered, "I've done all that in one year." It was a hectic time, but I really felt that our men's basketball and football programs were in excellent hands.

Chapter 9
The One and Only "Dream Team"

fter the 1984 Olympics, I was convinced that I
would never see another team as good as our gold-
medal team. At the time, of course, it was impossi-
ble to foresee the radical philosophical change that
enabled NBA stars to compete in the 1992 Games in
Barcelona, Spain. The media dubbed it the "Dream Team,"
and it was totally appropriate. Before our USA Basketball
committee selected the team, Charles Barkley came up to
me at the NBA All-Star Game and said, "Forget about 1984
... I want to be on this team." We didn't pick him in 1984
because he was out of shape. Although Charles did get em-
broiled in a couple of minor controversies, it didn't make
any difference because this was easily the best team the
world had ever seen. As Bill Wennington of the Canadian
team told *Sports Illustrated* before the Games, "The world
will end before the U.S. gets beaten."

Although I retired from coaching when I became the
Athletics Director at Kentucky, I continued to stay involved

with international basketball through my work with USA Basketball, the organization formerly known as ABAUSA. After serving as treasurer from 1984-88, I moved up to vice-president under my old friend Dave Gavitt from 1988-92. Then, after the Barcelona Games, I was picked to serve a four-year term as president. That would take me through the 1996 Olympics in Atlanta, and I thought it would more or less coincide with my retirement as athletics director at Kentucky. But for reasons that I'll discuss later, it didn't quite work out that neatly.

My interest in international basketball is partly selfish. Evelyn and I always have enjoyed traveling, so it's a way for someone who doesn't have a lot of money to see the world and enjoy other cultures. Beyond that, however, I wanted to do something to change the good ol' boy mentality that had dominated international basketball. Instead of being controlled mainly by Europe and America, the Federation of International Basketball Associations (FIBA) needed to become more global. It also needed to work to build up women's basketball. So there was the chance to be a catalyst for change, which appealed to me.

Finally, and I don't mean to sound self-serving, but I've always felt the need to give something back to the coaching profession. I've always felt that at the uppermost levels, athletes and coaches tend to be takers instead of givers. But I've gotten so much from basketball that I've tried to do anything I can to give something back in the hope of doing a bit of role-modeling or mentoring with younger coaches. They could maybe look at me and say, "Well, here's a guy who's very busy, but he's making time to promote international basketball." It did take time, not to mention a lot of energy, but I never let it detract from my duties at Kentucky. I never forgot where my paycheck was coming from.

It's not true that USA Basketball turned to the NBA players because we felt that we could no longer win international competitions with all-amateur teams. That kind of thinking probably began when we lost the 1987 Pan American Games to Brazil in Indianapolis. Then it really intensified after our 1988 Olympic team could do no better than a bronze medal in Seoul, our worst showing since men's basketball became an Olympic sport in 1936. At that point there was no question that the rest of the world had caught up. The gap had been closed. Anytime we played the Soviets or the Spanish or the Brazilians or others, we couldn't take victory for granted.

Even so, when open competition came up for a vote at the 1990 FIBA Congress in Barcelona, Dave Gavitt and I, representing USA Basketball, voted against it. So did the Soviet Union. But we were outvoted by the rest of the members for a couple of self-serving reasons. First, they were tired of losing to our amateur teams. Their thinking seemed to be that if they had to lose, they'd rather lose to the best players in the world. Second, there were economic

reasons. They could see our NBA stars helping them promote and market basketball in their countries.

I was against the idea because I still thought the
Olympics should be for amateurs. But I was as wrong as I
could be. Although I still think we could put together amateur teams that would be very competitive around the
world — not always victorious, but always competitive —
I now think that every citizen should be eligible to represent our country in the Olympics, even the ones who are
making a zillion dollars a year and are more famous than
movie stars. So letting the NBA stars participate was exactly the right thing to do. But once it was mandated that
you do it, the big question then became how to do it. For
the first time, the NBA and the NCAA would get together
to evaluate talent and pick a team.

Happily for all concerned, there wasn't nearly as much ac-
rimony as might have been expected. That was due to a lot
of hard work by men such as George Killian, a past president
of USA Basketball and FIBA; NBA Commissioner David Stern
and his deputy, Russ Granik; and Dave Gavitt, who had credentials as a college coach, conference commissioner and
vice-president of the Boston Celtics. They all worked to
overcome the paranoia in the minds of some that the NBA
would gobble up amateur basketball in this country.

It was a tremendous learning experience for everyone involved. We had to develop mutual understanding and trust

at all levels — NBA, college, junior college, AAU. We had to change the whole model for how the Olympic team is selected. And now, after a long history of four-year cycles in the selection process, we had a two-year cycle. When Dave made me responsible for putting the team together, we selected strong people from the NBA and the college ranks. The committee members were Bob Bass, Quinn Buckner, P.J. Carlesimo, Billy Cunningham, Wayne Embry, Charles Grantham, Mike Krzyzewski, Jack McCloskey, George Raveling, Rod Thorn, Jan Volk and Donnie Walsh. On both sides, there had to be a lot of give and take.

Our first and most important item of business was to select a head coach and staff to work with the committee. One of the stipulations was that the head coach would not select the team. Chuck Daly of the Detroit Pistons, who had coached at both the college and NBA levels, was the perfect choice as head coach. He had the respect of the players, a great sense of how to work with people and a laid-back, but organized, personality. For his assistants, we picked Lenny Wilkens, P.J. Carlesimo and Mike Krzyzewski.

Then we had to determine whether or not to have trials. We agreed that we couldn't ask NBA superstars to try out, so we decided to just pick the best team we could put together. We talked about quotas because, if we just picked the 12 best players, they all would come from the NBA. We finally decided that we needed some college representation, even if it was only one player. So that's how Christian Laettner of Duke became the team's only college player. Had I known what was going to happen in the final of the 1992 NCAA East Regional, I might have voted against him. I'm kidding, of course, although Laettner's miraculous turnaround jumper in overtime to beat Rick Pitino's third Kentucky team was a dagger in our hearts. But Christian deserved to be on the "Dream Team" because he had a lot of experience in international competition and he was a versatile big man. We wanted as much flexibility in terms of positions as we could possibly get.

Picking the team was a fascinating experience. We spent hours and hours, talking and arguing. We picked our centers first, putting all the names on the board. I remember looking up and thinking, "My goodness, how can we pick only two off that list?" But we ended up with Patrick Ewing of the New York Knicks and David Robinson of the San Antonio Spurs. Then we went to power forward. Our picks were Karl Malone of the Utah Jazz and Charles Barkley, who then was with the Philadelphia 76ers. Laettner came in later because he could play both center and power forward.

When we got to small forward, it really got crazy. We had all kinds of terrific choices, but we finally picked Larry Bird of the Boston Celtics and Scottie Pippen of the world-champion Chicago Bulls. At off guard, Michael Jordan of the Bulls was a no-brainer. Since our experience together at the 1984 Olympics, Michael had become the world's best and most popular player. To back him up, we picked Clyde Drexler of the Portland Trail Blazers. At point guard, we selected Magic Johnson, even though he had retired from the Los Angeles Lakers after testing HIV positive, and John Stockton of the Jazz. We also added Chris Mullin of the Golden State Warriors, who could play both off guard and small forward, because of his outside shooting ability. Bird was having trouble with his back, and we felt we might see a lot of zone defense.

When we got through and looked up at the board, I thought, "My God, look at the people we're leaving off this team ... You could have an incredible second or third or fourth team with the guys we left off."

There was some feeling in the media that some NBA players might not want to play for fear of injury or damaging their reputations, but that wasn't even a part of our selection process. We decided to invite a player and, if he turned us down, we'd move on down the line until we had a team. But we also decided that we would deal strictly with the players, not their agents. Happily for us, the excitement was there. Nobody turned us down. The players from our 1984 team — Jordan, Ewing and Mullin — were eager to have the experience again. But they were no more excited than the players who never had the opportunity to play in the Olympics simply because they had graduated, or turned pro, at the wrong time.

The NBA has the best marketing arm in pro sports and,

as soon as we announced the "Dream Team" on national TV in September 1991, the hype began. A story in *Sports Illustrated* reported that 40 companies were spending approximately $40 million in promotion and advertising to be involved with the team. The list included Nike, McDonald's, Coca-Cola and many other big names. All this interest proved to be profitable, in more ways than financial, for both USA Basketball and the NBA. As Russ Granik told *SI*, "Obviously, the Olympics will go a long way toward enhancing the NBA's business internationally."

After practicing together for a few days in San Diego, the "Dream Team" went to the Tournament of the Americas, an Olympic qualifying event in Portland, Ore. We won six games by an average of 51.5 points. Then it was on to Monte Carlo for a pre-Olympic training "camp" where more time was devoted to recreational and family activities than to basketball. When the team finally arrived in Barcelona, the reception was unbelievable. It surpassed anything we expected. Everywhere our players went, they were treated like rock stars. To get some privacy and rest, they stayed in hotels instead of the Olympic Village. Looking back on my 1984 experience, I think the 1992 team missed something there, but it was understandable. We insisted, however, that they march in the opening ceremony, something else that I remembered fondly from 1984, and they loved it.

Of all the things Evelyn and I have ever done together, I

think this was the most fun we had ever experienced, beginning with Monte Carlo and carrying on to Barcelona. For the first time, I had a chance to enjoy the Olympics. We attended some of the swimming and diving, some of the track and field, some of the badminton and baseball. There was no pressure on anybody because our team was just so good. We breezed to the gold medal, beating Croatia, 117-85, in the gold-medal game. Before that game, I asked Chuck Daly, "What's the thing that you're proudest of?" He said, "That we've gotten through it without bruising too many egos." I thought that was a great statement.

The games were so one-sided that maybe it was a good thing we had Charles to create controversy. In our lopsided opening win over Angola, Charles was hissed and booed for elbowing one of their players. Then he got in trouble with the U.S. Olympic Committee for ghostwriting a column for *USA Today*. That's a no-no, so he had to give it up. And, naturally, he was in the middle of the big logo flap. Some team members who had endorsement contracts with Nike had problems with the Reebok logo on our uniforms and warmups. At the gold-medal ceremony, Charles and Michael both wrapped themselves in an American flag to cover the small Reebok label that appeared on the warmup suit. So did Magic Johnson, who had just announced a split with Converse. At least with the amateur players, we never had problems like that.

Overall, however, it couldn't have worked out better, and I hope we continue to send the best teams we can put together. If a player such as, say, Tim Duncan doesn't make it as a collegian, he can make it as a pro. It was just the right thing to do. But let me make one thing clear: The media called our next international team "Dream Team II," but that's not right. In my mind, there will always be only one team that deserves that name. I agree with Magic Johnson. Asked when there would be another team as good as that one, he said, "Nope, it'll never happen again. Or, if it does, you guys won't be around and neither will we."

Our women's team also won the gold, and that set up my campaign, as head of USA Basketball, to upgrade the women's part of it. The adoption of Title IX in 1972, which mandated equality for women in athletics at public institutions, changed a lot of things, as I had quickly learned in my job as athletics director at Kentucky.

In the summer of 1996, I experienced one of the proudest moments of my career when the U.S. men's and women's basketball teams won gold medals at the Olympic Games in Atlanta. It was my final year as president of USA Basketball, and it was the first Olympics held in the South, where I had lived and worked my entire life. Coach Wilkens and his staff did a great job with the men's team, which had a lot to do with us getting the 2002 World Championship Games in Indianapolis, the first time that important event will be held in the U.S. But, for the first time, the men were overshadowed by the women's team.

Going into the Games, it was not a given that the women would win the gold. But they did, and it was especially gratifying to me because we had made a high dollar commitment to the national team concept, having a coaching staff salaried for an entire year to prepare, and you don't know if it's going to work or not. But Tara VanDerveer and the women's committee just did a great job in every respect.

The team drew huge crowds and, as a direct result of winning the gold medal, two pro leagues for women were started. Our best players — Jennifer Azzi, Lisa Leslie, Rebecca Lobo, Sheryl Swoopes, Venus Lacy, and all the others — consistently showed on national TV, against teams at a very elite level, that there would be a market for women pros. So, finally, our elite women players didn't have to travel to Europe or the Far East to play pro ball. Now, instead, the foreign athletes were coming here to play.

Beyond that, that team gave young females some athletic role models that they had not previously had. Before that Olympics, my granddaughters — Martin's daughters Katie and Madison — had worn the replica jerseys of Michael Jordan and Reggie Miller. But now they wanted to wear the jerseys of Lisa Leslie and the others that came along. That's critical to the future of women's basketball, and I'm proud that it happened on my watch.

Chapter 10
The Challenges of a Modern A.D.

W hen I was a player and a young coach, the athletics director position at a lot of universities was filled by a coach who had been eased out. It was a kind of emeritus position, more like being a dean of a college. The administrative part of it wasn't that challenging. The coaches in the revenue sports — football and men's basketball — were essentially their own athletics directors. So the A.D. was left to do a lot of back-slapping, glad-handing and golf-playing with alumni, donors and boosters.

Kentucky may have been one of the exceptions. Bernie Shively, who was the university's athletics director from 1938 through 1967, was a football man who played with Red Grange, the famed "Galloping Ghost," at Illinois. He came to UK in 1927 as the line coach under Harry Gamage, and six years later was named head of the Physical Education Department. In 1938, "Shive," as he was known, succeeded Chet Wynne as athletics director. He coached track and baseball for several seasons and, in

1945, was the head football coach before turning the job over to Coach Bryant, who was lured away from Maryland.

During Shively's 29 years, the university doubled the size of Stoll Field to a capacity of around 37,000 and built Memorial Coliseum. But one of his main contributions was his strong connections to the NCAA. He served two terms as chairman of the University Division Basketball Tournament Committee and also was a member of the NCAA Executive Committee. He was one of the main reasons the NCAA repeatedly assigned regional tournaments to the university in the 1950s and '60s, in addition to bringing the Final Four to Louisville's Freedom Hall six times between 1958 and 1969.

In 1968, Shively was succeeded by one of my mentors, Harry Lancaster, who had been Coach Rupp's No. 1 assistant from 1948 through '67. Several times during his years as an assistant, Coach Lancaster was approached about becoming a head coach elsewhere. But because Coach Rupp saw to it that he was paid well and given a lot of responsibility, he decided that the top assistant's job at Kentucky was a better deal than being the head coach at most places. Those were the days, remember, when some SEC schools hadn't awakened to the idea that basketball could join football as a significant revenue-producer.

Probably the most traumatic thing that happened during Harry's tenure was Coach Rupp's forced retirement. On

Sept. 1, 1971, Coach Rupp reached the university's mandatory retirement age of 70. Dr. Otis Singletary, then the university president, informed him that the 1971-72 season would be his last. But Coach Rupp balked and, as the season went on, he let it be known that he thought an exception should be made in his case. A group of former players, including Dan Issel and Louie Dampier, supported him. A petition to keep Coach Rupp was circulated, and a lot of pressure was brought to bear upon Dr. Singletary and Harry Lancaster. It must have been tough for Harry, but he had no choice but to support the president. Sadly, this led to a rift between Coach Rupp and Coach Lancaster. In fact, they didn't speak, except to say "good morning," for more than five years.

Harry didn't stay on the job long, but he got a lot done. It was on his watch that Commonwealth Stadium was built and the groundwork for Rupp Arena was laid. He pretty much hand-picked his successor, Cliff Hagan, who had been one of my teammates on the 1951 NCAA championship team. After his retirement from pro ball, Cliff came back to Lexington and took a job with one of the banks. But Harry made him his assistant in 1972 and groomed him to be his replacement. When Harry retired in 1975, Cliff got the job and held it until Dr. Roselle replaced him in 1989 and brought me in. Cliff did a lot of good things, especially with the so-called "non-revenue" sports and with building new facilities, but he just couldn't survive the negative image that came to surround the men's basketball program in the 1980s because of various alleged NCAA rules violations.

I think the athletics director's job began to change at Kentucky and other places when universities made the business decision to financially separate the athletics department from the rest of the university. In order to keep the athletics department from draining money from the general fund, in other words, universities mandated that it should be financially self-supporting. There was both good and bad in this. The good was it allowed the athletics department to do some things that were different from the rest of the university. One example is coaches salaries. But it also put athletics across the street from the rest of the university, and it put tremendous pressure on the athletics director. Since I've been at Kentucky, our budget has escalated from $14 million a year to $36 million. We've added three sports. Where Bernie Shively supervised a maximum of 10 sports at the end of his era, we now have 22 varsity teams.

I've always been a supporter of Title IX, the federal law that mandates that public institutions must do the same for women, in terms of opportunities, teams and scholarships, as it does for men. I've always attempted to provide strong leadership on minority and women's issues. However, considering that most of the women's teams at any university don't make money, that creates a real challenge for an athletics director. Imagine a corporation where the CEO is told that of his 22 divisions, only two will make a profit, but he doesn't have the option of dropping any of them. It's a tough proposition, from a business standpoint, and that's why we've got the Big Ten model — where several of those schools have gone for business-types as athletics directors instead of picking a person who has gone through the college experience as a coach or administrator. And I think we're going to see more of the professional sports administrator, considering that sports management is a growing field.

A few points about what I've tried to do at Kentucky:

• I've attempted to narrow the chasm between academics and athletics. A lot of that goes back to my experience at Transylvania, where I was a part of the faculty. That's also why I wanted to be the unofficial vice-president for athletics, so I could sit in on staff meetings. We use the term "athletics department" here instead of Athletics Association. We're a part of the university team, and you have to put the team above yourself. So we adhere to the same budget restrictions and the same purchasing restrictions as any other department on campus.

• We want to have a broad-based program that meets the interest and abilities of our student-athletes. In order to meet the demands of Title IX, some universities had tried to balance the ratio between men and women by dropping men's sports programs. But I think that's unacceptable philosophically, just as I think it's unacceptable to not allow walk-ons in football just to maintain some proportion or quota. If we have a bona fide student who wants the football experience, we should give it to him. We want to be a flagship in our state by having teams that represent what's happening in the high school programs of Kentucky.

• The main thing I've tried to do is set the standard for athletic-academic balance. The primary purpose of a university, contrary to what some of our fans think, is education. Our mission at the University of Kentucky is education, research and service. So that's first and foremost with me. In football, Jerry Claiborne set a high standard in academics that Bill Curry and Hal Mumme have strived to maintain. In basketball, it's a bit trickier because we've had several players who were good enough to leave school early for the NBA. I received some criticism when I had Sean Woods' jersey taken down from the rafters at Rupp Arena. But since Sean didn't leave school early and hasn't had a pro career, I see no reason why he hasn't gotten his degree. We've also told our coaches not to recruit players who can't do the work academically.

• We want to be compliant with the NCAA rules. It's well-documented that Kentucky has had problems in this area in the past, and we've had to do some education with some of our coaches in this area. You sometimes hear the argument that "other people are doing it," and that type of thing. That's why bringing in John Bostick was so important. I think the best thing about our success in football and men's basketball in the '90s is that we haven't had any trouble with the NCAA. As I've said going back to my days at Transylvania, winning isn't important unless it's done the right way. I thought we did a good thing by taking our coaches out of the entrepreneurial business. With us handling all that, they don't have to worry about car or clothes deals. We don't want our coaches beholden to any boosters, which has been a problem in the past. Rick Pitino was really great about that. Now we don't let people in our locker rooms and practices who don't belong there.

• We want to provide the support and expertise necessary to free up our coaches to do their job with young people. We try to put our student-athletes at the heart of the program. Our academic support program, CATS, has been very effective in helping student-athletes deal with their challenges. And, let's face it, the kids evaluate us just as we evaluate them. A player has a right to look at a coach or administrator and ask questions. Am I playing better as a junior than I did as a sophomore? Do they really put their money where their mouth is? Do they listen to students? I see my job as the one who sets that tempo on a daily basis. The rest of it is crisis management, going from one issue to another.

We've tried to talk to our athletes about the importance of giving back. If they're gifted, we spoil them from the highly organized youth programs on up. So we established mentoring programs, mostly through our Americare program, where we promote the real meaningful way to give back. That's one of the reasons Jamal Mashburn not only has given us his time and talents when we've asked, but also why he gave us $500,000 to help underprivileged youngsters. Rex Chapman also has given us some dollars. To give back is an important thing for successful people in every walk of life. I was pleased to see that Charles Barkley donated some money to Auburn and his high school. Eventually, I think, Charles will retract his statement about not wanting to be anybody's role model.

When you get right down to it, being an athletics director is like coaching. You're in the people business. With people like me and Vince Dooley of Georgia and Doug Dickey of Tennessee, we had to do a lot of on-the-job training. When I took this job, I told Larry Ivy, "Don't let me screw it up financially." And sometimes I still tell Dr. Wethington, "I'd lose a lot of sleep if I were you, having an old basketball coach in charge of a $36 million budget." I suppose the big difference is that coaching is more measurable. You've got your won-lost record, how far you went in the tournament, how close your team came to reaching its potential. But an A.D.'s job is so big and so diverse that you can't measure success so easily. You've got to make a decision, do it for the right reasons, and hope for the best. And as I've said earlier, you've got to be willing to take a risk.

Which brings me around to how I became the first UK athletics director to hire an African-American men's basketball coach and the first SEC athletics director to hire a head football coach from Division II.

Chapter 11
It Took a Special Coach to Replace Rick Pitino

W hen we hired Rick Pitino, we gave him a seven-year contract. Normally, you figure it would take a coach five years to build a Final Four team, but we gave Rick two extra years because we thought it would take at least that long, considering the terms of our NCAA probation, to get the program back to where it was at least competitive. You talk about taking a risk. That's what Rick did when he came to the university in 1989. But he thrives on challenges, and there was none bigger than picking up the pieces at Kentucky.

He went 14-14 his first season with one of the least physically talented teams in the university's history. In retrospect, that may have been his best coaching job. By the end of his third year, the team was good enough to take eventual NCAA champion Duke into overtime. Only that miraculous turnaround jumper by Christian Laettner kept us out of the Final Four. A year later, our 1992-93 team made the Final Four. It was one of the most amazing rebuilding jobs I had ever seen.

On the night of April 1, 1996, we reached the pinnacle during the final year of Rick's original seven-year contract, beating Syracuse, 76-67, in the NCAA championship game at the Meadowlands to give the university its sixth national title and its first since 1978. I enjoyed every minute of that evening, and I felt especially grateful to Rick for the job he had done.

I think there are several reasons why he was such a special coach for us. First, he's a great teacher, both in the individual skills and the team part of it. Second, he's a great communicator with the players. They know where they stand and where he stands. He motivated some players with fear, as Coach Rupp did, and others with hugs, but he also seemed to hit the right note with every player. Third, he's very innovative both offensively and defensively. He's a basketball purist, a basketball junkie. Just the hardest-working guy I've ever been around and it carried over to his teams. Finally, he was truly an educator. He wanted his players to be good people and to do well in school.

Rick is so intense and confident that some outsiders probably figure he was difficult to work with. But that simply was never the case. He'd push for things he thought were important, but he could take "no" for an answer and then it was over. He's very high-energy and he's an idea guy. He told me that he kept yellow legal pads on his bed-side table so he could jot down ideas when they came to him during the night. Sometimes I'd tell him, when he was trying to push an idea, "I'm going to destroy all those yel-low pads." But Rick was a joy to be around, and I'll always value that relationship.

So after we beat Syracuse to win the title, it was just a great feeling to be back after all the stuff that had gone on in the past. Under Dr. Roselle's leadership, we had created the model of handling an NCAA investiga-tion and doing it right. And now we were there, back at the top. To me the best thing was that there was no hol-lowness in this championship. I felt good for the uni-versity, for the Commonwealth, for our players and coaches and for the fans who had hung with us during the tough times. Nobody really made much of it at the time, but that '96 championship team also was the first Kentucky team to have five black starters — Antoine Walker, Tony Delk, Walter McCarty, Anthony Epps and Derek Anderson.

During Rick's stay in Lexington, it seemed rumors of his return to the NBA would surface at the conclusion of each season. It became a rite of spring in Kentucky. But I never worried about it because I felt there was only one pro team that Rick would leave Kentucky for — the Boston Celtics. He's a traditionalist, and the Celtics are to the NBA what Kentucky is to college basketball. Plus, he went to college at UMass, and coached at Boston University and Providence. He and Joanne like that area and feel at home there.

During the 1996-97 season, Rick did another fantastic job. Despite losing three starters from the championship team as well as Derek Anderson to a knee injury in January, he took us back to the NCAA title game in the RCA Dome in Indianapolis. We lost in overtime to Arizona, 84-79, but it still was a great season. Even Rick's detractors had to admit that he was the hottest coach in college basketball.

Rick and I always had an agreement about coaching opportunities. He told me, "If I ever get serious about a job, you'll hear about it right then. But until you hear it from me, don't pay any attention to anything you might hear or read." When the Celtics contacted him shortly after the 1997 title game, he came to me and said he was going to talk to the owner. "But I'm not going anywhere," he said. Right then I thought to myself, "You might not know it yet, but I think this is the one you're going to take." Sure enough, after much agonizing back and forth, he told me he was going to accept the Celtics offer. I told him, "I hate to see you leave, but I understand and I thank you for what you've done for the university and the state."

I really meant that. I felt that Rick had given us the best eight years of his coaching life. When he took the job, we were in such a mess that, for the first time ever, the Kentucky job wasn't considered to be a plum. But when he left, we were back in the position where we could pretty much hire anybody we wanted. The people in the state always should feel indebted to Rick. The Celtics were in disarray, just as we had been when Rick came along, and I know the idea of restoring them to glory was exactly the sort of challenge that he thrives on.

Right away I had three or four names that I seriously thought about. I'm a great one for putting things down on a yellow legal pad, then listing the pluses and minuses. Every time I did that, one name emerged — Tubby Smith. The main reason was that he had gone into Tulsa and Georgia, programs that had enjoyed success through the years, and not been fazed by the expectations. The most difficult thing a coach can be asked to do is go into a program that has great expectations and try to meet those expectations with players he didn't recruit. And it would be quadrupally difficult trying to follow Rick Pitino at Kentucky. But I thought, "If we get the right guy, we won't miss a beat here." And I was convinced that Tubby was the right guy because of his experience, his style of play and the high-quality person that he is. I've always tried not to put a player or a coach in a no-win situation.

215

That's why I never recruited a player who I didn't think could graduate. But I was confident Tubby would be a winner at Kentucky.

Of course, I thought about the fact that he would be Kentucky's first African-American men's basketball coach, but that was pretty much a non-issue with me. We already had a black women's coach in Bernadette Mattox. I figured Tubby would be fine if we made it clear to him that we were going to protect him unconditionally and that he would have our total support. Before we closed the deal, a black columnist for the *Lexington Herald-Leader*, Merlene Davis, wrote a column urging Tubby not to take the job because she didn't believe Lexington was ready to accept a black men's basketball coach. That upset me because of the timing. Had she written it after we hired Tubby, that would have been fine. But to write it while we were in the process and to have that faxed to him by Georgia fans, well, that bothered me. But Tubby took the job because he really wanted to be here. That was important. I didn't want anybody who didn't want to be here.

I didn't think hiring Tubby was a big risk on our part, even though I knew the national media would jump all over the idea of an African-American having the job that once belonged to Coach Rupp. Sure enough, that's what happened. They drug out all the old charges — untrue charges, I believe — about Coach Rupp being a racist and all that.

But Tubby handled it beautifully and stayed focused. He had enough on his plate with trying to follow Rick and meet the expectations. It was a tremendous risk on Tubby's part to take the job, but he was willing to step up to the plate and take the risk.

Nobody could have anticipated what happened in the magical season of 1997-98. Although we had lost Derek Anderson and Ron Mercer to the NBA — both were first-round draft choices — Tubby put together an over-achieving team that came together late in the regular season. Early in the season, one of our players commented publicly that we should be pressing more or running more. Naturally, the radio call-in shows picked up on that. But I really admired how Tubby handled that. He kept his cool and gradually won the players over. The catalysts were senior guard Jeff Sheppard and junior forward Scott Padgett. But Nazr Mohammed, who was little more than a project when Rick recruited him out of Chicago, blossomed into one of the nation's finest centers. And Cameron Mills, a pure shooter if there ever was one, always provided a big lift off the bench. By the postseason, they were playing incredibly hard for Tubby, even though there wasn't an All-American in the bunch. In three SEC Tournament games and in the first three NCAA Tournament games, Kentucky's margins of victory were 11, 25, 30, 15, 27 and 26.

That put us in the South Regional championship game against Duke. It was our first game against the Blue Devils since the classic in the '92 East Regional final, and this one was every bit as thrilling — more so, if you were a Kentucky fan. In the final 9:38, our players erased a 17-point deficit to win, 86-84, and put us in the Final Four for the third consecutive year. At the Alamodome in San Antonio, we defeated Stanford in overtime, 86-85, and Utah in the title game, 78-69. Tubby Smith had become the first coach to win the NCAA title in his first year at a school since Ed Jucker did it at Cincinnati in 1961. Frankly, under the circumstances, I thought it was one of the greatest coaching jobs I had ever seen.

As the chairman of the NCAA Division I Men's Basketball Committee, it was my job to present the championship trophy to the winning coach. Before we went on the platform that had been set up on the court, I thanked Tubby for taking the job and for the great job he had done, and I told him how proud I was of him. Then came the presentation. Of all the things that have excited me in sports, next to winning the Olympic gold medal, this was the best. It just doesn't get any better and I couldn't have been any happier. With Tubby in charge, Kentucky basketball will be in good hands for years to come.

But all the ecstasy that I had derived from our basketball success was balanced by the agony I felt in dealing with the Bill Curry situation in football.

NEWTON'S LAWS

C.M. with golf partner Bob Knight.

Former Vanderbilt Athletics Director and current Southeastern Conference Commissioner Roy Kramer congratulates C.M. on his 500th victory as a head coach on Jan. 21, 1989.

Frances and Cawood Ledford look up to the rafters of Rupp Arena along with C.M. as a banner honoring the "Voice of the Wildcats" is unveiled.

The Fabulous Five Reunion: Humzey Yessin, Ralph Beard, Alex Groza, Kenny Rollins, Wah Wah Jones, Joe Holland, Buddy Parker and Dale Barnstable.

With a UK pin on Rick Pitino's lapel, C.M. had his coach.

C.M. and former UK coach Rick Pitino share a light moment during practice.

C.M. presides as UK President Charles Wethington officially makes Tubby Smith the Wildcat coach in 1997.

As chair of the NCAA Division I Men's Basketball Committee, C.M. had the pleasure of presenting Tubby Smith and the Wildcats with the 1998 championship trophy.

The 1984 USA Olympic Men's Basketball Team.
Front Row (L-R): Steve Alford, Leon Wood,
Michael Jordan, Alvin Robertson, Vern Fleming.
Back Row: C.M. Newton, Bob Knight, Tim Garl,
Wayman Tisdale, Jeff Turner, Patrick Ewing,
Jon Koncak, Joe Kleine, Sam Perkins,
Chris Mullin, George Raveling, Don Donoher.

As President of USA Basketball, C.M. and the U.S.
squad were good as gold during the 1996 Olympic
Games in Atlanta.

C.M. shares a moment with U.S.
players Karl Malone, Penny Hardaway
and Charles Barkley.

The "Dream Team"

C.M. with close friend John McMahon.

C.M. receives the regional Athletics Director of the Year award from the National Association of Collegiate Directors of Athletics in 1999.

C.M. with former Tennessee coach Ray Mears.

Front Row (L-R): Dave Gavitt, Henry Iba, Pete Newell, Dean Smith. Back Row: George Raveling, Bob Knight, C.M. Newton, Don Donoher.

*C.M. receiving an honorary
degree from Centre College.*

Katie, Martin, Zach, Cindy and Madison.

C.M. with Richard Sterban
of the Oak Ridge Boys.

At the 1999 Kentucky Derby
with (L-R): Donnie McCammon,
Bill Bryan, Becky Bryan, C.M.,
Cindy Newton, Martin Newton,
Pat Host and Jim Host.

Bill Bryan, Becky Bryan, Ruth Newton,
Evelyn Newton and Richard Newton.

Deborah Newton

Richard Newton

Col. R.Y. Newton III

Katie

Madison

Zach

Phil, Tracy and Sheridan Chappelle.

Katie, C.M., Madison, Zach and Martin Newton.

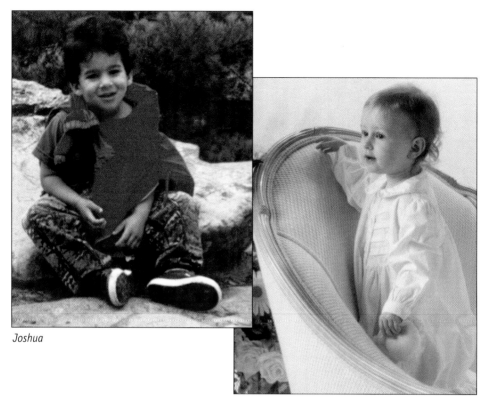

Joshua

Sheridan

1988 family reunion.

Evelyn and C.M.

Bone fishing in the Bahamas.

C.M. presents former Kentucky
Governor A.B. "Happy" Chandler
with an award.

C.M. with Jeff Turner, one of his stars at Vanderbilt and a member
of the 1984 U.S. Olympic team.

Chapter 12
How a Mumme Breathed Life Into UK Football

When I took the job at Kentucky, I told Dr. Roselle I would give him seven good years. My thinking was that I would retire in the spring of 1996 because that would coincide with the Olympics and the end of my presidency of USA Basketball. Evelyn and I would still be young enough to try some of the things we never had a chance to do. For example, I've always thought I would like to try painting. I've got these pictures of bonefish flats stored in my head, and I'd like to see if I could put them on canvas. But in good conscience, I felt I couldn't leave until we got our football program on solid ground.

When I hired Bill Curry, I was confident he would be such a great fit with what we wanted to accomplish. When we went to the Peach Bowl in 1993, Bill's fourth year, I thought we were very much on schedule. But then we dropped to 1-10 in 1994 and 4-7 in 1995. Even more important than that, the fun had gone out of our football program. I'm still not sure what went wrong and why. I still think Bill is an outstanding football coach. And even more, an outstanding person. I've searched for the answers as to why it didn't work at Kentucky the way it worked at Georgia Tech and Alabama. But I can't find an answer, except at Kentucky you have no margin for error. Anyway, I wanted to be sure, because of the respect I had for Bill as a coach and a person, that he had every opportunity to make this thing go.

Entering the 1996 season, there was a lot of excitement around the state because Bill had been able to recruit Tim Couch, the phenomenal high school quarterback from Hyden, Ky., who could have gone to Tennessee or Florida State or anywhere he wanted. But Bill's offensive coordinator, Elliot Uzelac, decided to go with an option attack with Billy Jack Haskins at quarterback. That left Couch on the bench. When he got an opportunity to play he operated an offense that wasn't suited to him. A lot of people felt that the Couch thing was the final straw that led me to terminate Bill's contract, but that's not true. That was a coach's decision, not an athletics director's decision.

After we lost to LSU, 41-14, in Baton Rouge on Saturday, Oct. 19, I decided we had to make a change. Our only victory in our first seven games was an uninspiring 3-0 win over Indiana at Commonwealth Stadium. Louisville and Cincinnati had drilled us. Florida had whipped us 65-0 in Gainesville. Making that decision was one of the most difficult things I've ever had to do, other than some family issues. Evelyn and I were close to Bill and his wife Carolyn, just as we were with Rick and Joanne Pitino. It was difficult not only on Bill, but on his family and my family. I'm happy to say that to this day that we're still good friends and we'll always care about each other.

My experience as a coach helped me to not only know it was time to make a change, but how I would handle it. I just didn't feel I could do what a lot of athletics directors do. That is, I can't publicly act like I'm supporting somebody at the same time I'm secretly beginning a search for a new coach. So that Sunday night following the loss to LSU, I met Bill in his office and told him I felt like we needed to make a change, that it just wasn't going to work and we needed to make the change so we would be freed up to find another coach and not lose a recruiting year.

I asked him to resign in the hope we could announce it as a mutual decision. He said he wanted to think about it. So later that night, I went over to his house and he told me, "I've told these players to never give up ... that if you get knocked down, get back up ... so I can't in good conscience go against that by giving up." I understood what he was saying and respected him for it. That's one reason his players respected him so much — he practiced what he preached. Bill was the kind of person who believed that if you just worked hard enough, good things would eventually happen. But good things just didn't happen to Bill in this case. That was too bad because he loved it at the university and really believed in what we were doing.

He had concerns over the next day or so about being in a lame-duck situation, so I told him how I had handled it in my last year at Vanderbilt. The difference was that it was my decision to leave Vanderbilt and it wasn't Bill's decision to leave Kentucky. So I announced the decision on Monday, Oct. 21, and there was a heckuva risk in doing that. Bill could have decided to fight it publicly or he could have left right away or his team could have quit on him. These things can get very political, as everybody learned when Eddie Sutton tried to take on Dr. Roselle in 1989. But Dr. Wethington backed it and made the calls he had to make.

The rest of the way, Bill and his staff worked their fannies off and his players showed how much they respected Bill by playing hard every game. They beat Georgia, Mississippi State and Vanderbilt before getting bombed by Tennessee in Knoxville. I was proud of the way everybody handled a difficult situation. One positive thing about doing it when we did was that we were able to get a head start on finding new jobs for Bill's assistants. As for Bill, we honored his contract. We didn't try to negotiate down or anything like that. That's when you need a strong president to approve things like that, and Dr. Wethington agreed with me that we would treat Bill as honorably as we possibly could.

So while Bill's career was winding down with as much dignity as could be mustered under the circumstances, I started the search for a new coach. Contrary to popular belief, Kentucky has a strong football fan base and we have facilities that are second to none. So I was confident I could find a good coach. I'm more knowledgeable about football than a lot of people think. Over the years, a lot of coaches who I respect have come into the SEC and coached their fannies off with old-fashioned, smash-mouth football, but they haven't been successful. So I decided to find somebody who could go about it a different way, who could be the football equivalent of Rick Pitino. In other words, I wanted someone who could press, fast-break and shoot the three on grass.

I looked at the NFL and came up with Sherman Lewis and Larry Kirksey, a couple of highly regarded assistants who had Kentucky roots. I looked at a couple of proven winners who were out of coaching at the time — Howard Schnellenberger, a UK alumnus who had won the 1983 national title at Miami, and Mike Gottfried, who had built a career as an ESPN analyst after building winners at Murray State, Kansas, Cincinnati and Pittsburgh. My list also included David Cutcliffe, the offensive coordinator at Tennessee, and Tommy Bowden, who had a great coaching pedigree. What all six had in common was that they believed in wide-open, offensive football.

I put another name on the list when I got a call from Carl Parker, who had played for Watson Brown at Vanderbilt when I was coaching basketball there. "I know how crazy you were about Watson's offensive schemes," Carl said, "so I just wanted to let you know that there's a coach at Valdosta State who's the most innovative offensive coach I've ever been around, including Watson." So that's how Hal Mumme came to my attention. I told Carl to see if Hal was interested and, if he was, to send me a résumé and the names of three football people I could call to check him out. "I don't want lawyers, ministers or college presidents on the list," I said. "I want football people." So I got Hal's list and his three names were LaVell Edwards, the coach at Brigham Young; Grant Teaff, the former coach at Baylor; and Larry Lacewell, who had been a head coach and assistant on both the college and NFL levels.

I decided I was going to spend a nickel to call these guys and ask them the $64,000 question: "Do you think Hal Mumme would be a good hire?" LaVell Edwards didn't hesitate. "Yes," he said, "because you're not going to win in that league knocking people off the football ... you've got to throw the ball." Grant Teaff said, "I don't know, but let me make a few phone calls and I'll get back to you." He called back and said, "C.M., Hal Mumme's your man." Larry Lacewell said pretty much the same thing. So I told our people, "Let's go see him and study this some more."

I personally interviewed all seven of the finalists. With each of them, I asked if they wanted their wives to sit in. When you hire a coach, you also hire the coach's wife. When I met with Hal, June sat in, and a one-hour visit turned into three. I asked each candidate, "What's the unique thing about you as a coach?" Most of them wanted to talk about their approach to recruiting or their offensive philosophy. But Hal said, "One thing I bring to the table is that I remember what it was like to be 19 years old." He said he had only one rule — don't do anything to hurt the team — and I liked that because I was never much on having a lot of rules. When we were done, Hal took Larry Ivy and I back to our plane. Before we got on, Hal said, "I have one more question: Do you really think you can hire a Division II coach at Kentucky?" I said, "Hal, if you're the right guy, I've got the balls to hire you."

We went back to see him again and we took some of our staff along. This time he said he wanted to bring his defensive coordinator, Mike Major, along with him. I thought that was pretty strong. Then we took Dr. Wethington to Valdosta to meet with him. After that, our committee got down to making the decision. Initially, there was some fairly strong feeling to go the safe route and hire Mike Gottfried, a proven winner at the Division I level and a well-known name because of his ESPN exposure. But I think they were really trying to protect me. The idea was,

"Don't make it your legacy to make a mistake by hiring a Division II coach." But the more we got into it, the more support surfaced for Hal. I finally decided that what LaVell Edwards said rang true. Plus, I had talked with Roy Kramer, who had left Vanderbilt to become the SEC commissioner, and he told me, "Football is football, and good coaches can come from anywhere."

That made me remember Coach Bryant had hired a no-name, small-college coach from Transylvania and that had worked out rather well. So why couldn't this work if Hal was the right guy? One thing I liked about Hal was that every place he had been, he had built programs the right way, starting from the ground up, instead of trying to get a quick fix with transfers. That really appealed to me and it ruled out some of the other guys. In addition, some of the candidates paid little attention to academics. When that question came up with Hal, June said, "If you really want to know about my husband, why don't you talk to some of his former players?" We did, and they all gave Hal ringing endorsements.

So I kind of made the decision to hire Hal the same way I made the decision to make Wendell Hudson the first black scholarship athlete at Alabama. I figured that if it didn't work, they would fire me anyhow, because I would be zip-for-two in hiring football coaches. I told Dr. Wethington that if Hal didn't work out, "I'll fire him, you fire me and then you go out and get an A.D. that will get you a football coach who knows how to get the job done." When I called Hal to offer him the job, he laughed and said, "Boy, you do have big balls, don't you?"

It would be an understatement to say I'm tickled with the way it's worked out. Hal recognized immediately that Tim Couch was the perfect quarterback to run his high-tech passing game, so he gave him the job even before spring practice began. That caused Billy Jack Haskins to transfer to Rhode Island, which I regretted, but it was the right thing for Hal to do. With Couch throwing the ball all over the place, we opened the season against the same Louisville team that had humiliated us the previous year and we beat them soundly. We were competitive in every game and the fans were really fired up about Hal's bold coaching style and Couch's passing. The final record was 5-6, but I'd have to say it was the most exciting 5-6 in Kentucky history. When we upset Alabama at Commonwealth Stadium, the crowd stormed the field and tore down the goal posts. It had been a long time since there had been that kind of excitement around Kentucky football.

The 1998 season was even better. Couch was so good that he became a finalist for the Heisman Trophy and, eventually, the No. 1 pick in the NFL draft. The team finished with a 7-4 record, our first winning season since 1989. We received an invitation to a New Year's Day bowl game, the Outback Bowl in Tampa, largely because the fans and the media had fallen in love with Tim's star quality and Hal's exciting offense. Although Penn State beat us, 26-14, there was no way we could come out of that game as losers. All the national publicity figured to help us expand our recruiting base. In addition, the excitement about Hal's program and our future enabled us to press ahead with our plans to expand and improve Commonwealth Stadium. At a cost of more than $24 million, we added 40 luxury boxes, two huge Diamond Vision video boards and increased the seating capacity from 57,800 to more than 68,000. In 1999, to the surprise of many, our team posted a 6-5 record and earned a berth against Syracuse in the Music City Bowl in Nashville. And a really great thing, from an A.D.'s standpoint, is that we sold out all available tickets except for student tickets and visiting-team tickets. As I told Hal after getting our second consecutive bowl bid, who would have "thunk" it?

So, finally, I was comfortable that we had the football program headed in the right direction. Heck, even those rascals in the media seemed excited and positive, and that's a rare condition for some of them.

Chapter 13
On the Record About the Media

O f all the changes I've seen in my 50 years in college athletics, the major one has been in the media. Right away I want it understood that I'm not a media-basher. The relationships I've had with the media, with one or two exceptions, have been good. I've always tried to understand that they have a tough job to do, just as I hope they understand I have a tough job to do. But mainly because of the growth in television at all levels — local, regional and national — the demands on the coaches and players have grown 110 percent since I was a player at Kentucky and a young coach at Transylvania. Inevitably, I suppose, these demands lead to a lot more confrontations involving coaches and/or players with the media. (Of course, those demands also have led to more confrontations between coaches and players.) We live in media-driven times where a lot of egos clash on a daily basis.

When TV was in its formative years in the early 1950s,

253

most cities, including Lexington, had at least two newspapers. The morning paper had the advantage of getting the first crack at the previous day's games and news events. The afternoon paper mainly specialized in follow-ups, features and looking ahead. If you were a fan, you would attend a game or listen to it on the radio, then look forward to reading about it in the next day's papers. Most newspapers, especially those located in smaller cities, didn't do too much investigative-type reporting. This was especially true in sports, where writers tended to be fans of the home team. I'm not saying this is necessarily good, but it certainly made for better relationships between coaches and writers.

As the electronic media expanded, many newspapers died. So today the competition isn't so much one paper against another, but the print media against the electronic media. And where big-city, syndicated newspaper columnists used to carry the most weight — Coach Rupp used to love to wine and dine those fellows when Kentucky played in New York — now national TV commentators such as Dick Vitale and Billy Packer are far more influential than any newspaper columnist. Sometimes I wonder if the newspaper folks get so jealous about the celebrity status of guys like Vitale and Packer that they'll tend to dig up controversial stuff just for the sake of drawing attention to themselves.

It's easy to measure how the media has grown and

changed. In 1957-58, the season that Coach Rupp won his fourth NCAA title with the team known as the "Fiddlin' Five," the media guide listed the following outlets who covered the team on a regular basis: 10 newspapers, two wire services (Associated Press and United Press), 11 radio stations and two TV stations. By the 1998-99 season, those numbers had increased to 26 newspapers, six radio stations or networks and 16 TV stations. And this doesn't count the national TV networks and publications that cover us on a fairly regular basis. But where the number of major daily newspapers has decreased (Lexington and Louisville now have only one daily) and the radio has been consolidated into the UK network (in the 1950s we had as many as five stations or networks originating play-by-play), television, with all its attendant space and equipment requirements, has proliferated.

My main concern always has been for the players. I can't image what it must be like to be an 18- or 19-year old boy and having all those cameras and microphones thrust in your face on a daily basis. Heck, when I played, we had very little contact with the media. Coach Rupp wouldn't even allow reporters in the locker room after games. About the only coach who gets away with that today is Bob Knight of Indiana, which probably is one of the reasons he has such a negative image with many members of the media. I understand there's a certain amount of glamour attached to being treated as a celebrity — when I was at Transylvania, for example, our players would have given anything to get just a fraction of the publicity that routinely went to the UK players — but it's also a double-edged sword. A Kentucky player lives in a fishbowl and, when he messes up, he gets far more scrutiny than a normal student who made the same mistake.

With many coaches and players, the intense media competition almost becomes a game within the game, and you have to decide who you can trust and who you can't. There was a time when a coach could sit down with certain writers and talk candidly because it was completely understood that everything was off the record. I'm talking about men such as Tom Siler in Knoxville, Fred Russell in Nashville, Mike McKenzie in Tuscaloosa and Alf Van Hoose and Clyde Bolton in Birmingham. But today, by and large, coaches and journalists just don't have that kind of relationship. Heck, coaches don't even have that level of trust among themselves.

When I was first coaching in the SEC, I'd go out and have dinner with Coach Rupp or Press Maravich at LSU and others. We would always talk about the game: rules, offense and defense, how to coach and how to play. But today the conversation would be about stock options, sneaker contracts, how much money they're making off their TV and radio shows. Of course, I don't think coaches socialize nearly as much as they used to. So if a level of trust doesn't exist there, how can it exist between coaches and journalists? The central issue, I'm sure, is control. A relationship must be based on mutual trust, respect and understanding, but there are control issues that inevitably create a conflict. We want to determine what's news and when it's released. But everybody in the media is so competitive and so afraid of getting beat on a story that their agenda often is in direct conflict with ours. It's a problem, and I just don't know the answer to it.

I also believe that sports editors don't have the autonomy they used to have. These days a lot of stories originate at the level of a higher editor, maybe even the publisher. In the fall of 1999, for example, the *Lexington Herald-Leader* decided it wanted to do an evaluation of our zero-tolerance alcohol policy regarding student-athletes on its one-year anniversary. Our feeling was that we wanted to do that ourselves, internally, at the proper time. We would look at it and get input and tweak it, if necessary. So when the *Herald-Leader* sent a reporter to talk to me, I told him, "If you want to know if our policy is working, let's wait until we have a chance to evaluate it." We told him that, at the appropriate time, we would make one athlete and one coach available from each sport. But he said the paper was going ahead, so we decided not to let him talk to our players and coaches. They ended up talking to a professor and a tavern owner. But I didn't blame the reporter. He was just a messenger, the middle man. He didn't have the autonomy to make a publishing decision. Again, I guess it's about control.

In recent years, my biggest beef with the print media has been the daily printing of the Las Vegas gambling line on college games. The whole issue with me is one of integrity. Betting on sports, while it's socially acceptable, is against the law, and I have a difficult time understanding why a newspaper would promote something that's against the law. I don't think a newspaper would accept classified ads for the sale of heroin or cocaine. So why would it print the gambling line? Their counter-argument is that the public wants to know who the favorite is and by how many points, and I'm sure there would be a hue and cry if papers stopped printing the line. But I still think it promotes illegal gambling.

I feel so strongly about it that, a few years ago, I was part of a group on the NCAA Tournament Committee that floated the idea of withholding credentials from any newspaper or radio-TV station that distributed the Vegas line. If that meant the only paper that covered the Final Four was *The New York Times*, so be it. Well, I lost that battle, but I refuse to give up the fight against anything that promotes gambling on college sports. I'm not trying to lead the world on an anti-gambling crusade, but I do want to make a difference in the lives of our student-athletes.

I remember one game when we got a big lead. Rick Pitino took out our starters, but the other coach kept his in. They cut into our margin, although the outcome was never in doubt, but out of our student section came a chorus of boos.

"What's that all about?" Evelyn asked me.

"Honey," I said, "it's the line … those are gamblers."

"Our students?" she said, horrified.

Studies have shown that we have a huge problem today with student bookmakers and student gambling. In every point-shaving scandal we've ever had in college basketball, student bookmakers have been involved. It really bothers me, because I know first-hand, going back to the scandal at Kentucky during my playing days, how gambling can ruin lives and careers. And now, because of the Internet, students can even gamble from their rooms, if they know how. That really scares me.

One of the real benefits to the SEC was the early work of Bob Barrett, a former FBI agent who was in charge of compliance for the league. Bob has since retired, but one thing he did was keep his own line on games involving conference teams. If he saw any kind of change in a pattern, he would let a school know. It's been really good for me to be able to pick his brain on gambling and sports betting. Because of his expertise, the SEC was one of the first conferences to do serious background checks on game officials. Bob Barrett has important insights and he's way ahead of his time in terms of understanding the potential for disaster that's inherent in sports gambling.

I can't say for sure that the presence of the Vegas line in newspapers has promoted illegal gambling, but newspapers are able to get away with it because gambling has become socially acceptable. In Kentucky, we have horse racing, a lottery, riverboat casinos and off-track betting parlors. I'm sure it's difficult for a lot of youngsters to understand the difference, morally, between buying a lottery ticket and betting on a game. I hope we can convince the media to at least understand the seriousness of the problem and join in trying to educate the public about the perils of sports gambling.

I was really gratified by a move the *Herald-Leader* made in the fall of 1999. They were running this little box with stories about our football games that had our helmet and the helmet of our opponent atop some vital information about the game. One of the "facts" was the point spread. I had a meeting with Pam Luecke, the editor of the *Herald-Leader*, and I told her, "We're going to insist that you either remove the gambling line from that box or you remove our helmet logo. Let's not put an illegal factor into the game facts." To my pleasant surprise, she agreed. I was really appreciative of her understanding and cooperation.

One fairly new aspect of the media that troubles me is the radio call-in show. Coaches profit handsomely from the revenue they receive from their radio and TV shows, and part of the deal is that they have to take questions from the public. But the thing that bothers me is that the callers have anonymity. They can say anything they want and not be held accountable for it. I don't think coaches mind tough questions about personnel or strategy, provided they come from people with a certain amount of expertise. They know they have to be responsible for their decisions and accountable to the public. But when it gets to be a feeding frenzy as it often does after a tough loss, that's when you get anonymous callers who are rude and ugly.

I wish radio stations would adopt a policy similar to the one that many newspapers have about letters to the editor. They insist that the letters must be signed, and then they double-check to make certain the writer actually exists and lives where he says he does. They also don't print letters that contain factual inaccuracies and irresponsible comments. Isn't there a way radio stations could do that? But every time I get disgusted by a call-in show, I also think of all the free publicity that we derive from them. As I said earlier, it's a double-edged sword.

However, I have absolutely no ambivalence over the recruiting newsletters that have proliferated as college basketball has evolved into a national sport. That whole phenomenon is interesting, for lack of a better word. You've got some guys who, by and large, couldn't hack it at a regular newspaper. So they become recruiting "gurus" and start up these newsletters and Internet websites that pander to the unquenchable thirst that certain fans have for gossip about where high school players are going to attend college. What's really ridiculous is when they get into ranking the top 100 or 150 players at every position, or the top 100 sophomores, freshmen, eighth-graders, etc. They're creating a false image and a false sense of values for these players at a very young age. Suddenly a lot of these youngsters begin thinking they're the next Michael Jordan or Tim Duncan. Maybe they are, but the odds are great that they're not.

So when the recruiting process starts, these pampered prospects bring a lot of unfortunate baggage to the table. They've been told how good they are for so long that they've come to believe it. Many of them have a street agent telling them one thing, an AAU coach telling them something else and their parents pushing them in another direction. In my opinion, these recruiting "gurus" are parasites who damage a lot of kids by creating false hopes. They've made the whole recruiting process infinitely more difficult and unappealing for a lot of coaches. That's one reason I think we need to go back to freshman ineligibility. That would give a student-athlete some breathing room to adjust to college. It also would weed out the players who have neither the interest nor the ability to do college academic work.

Finally, there's the whole business of our relationship with TV, which is a pretty delicate thing. There's no question that the over-proliferation of college games on TV has created a tremendous decline in attendance at the high-school level. It's not totally due to TV, but TV has certainly played a major part. It used to be that Tuesdays and Fridays were the high school nights, and we protected them by not playing on those nights. That's not the case anymore. Although consolidation has created bigger high schools in terms of enrollment, they don't get the following that the smaller schools received in the days before so many college games were on TV. If Duke is playing North Carolina on ESPN on a Friday night, you might get 200 people for a high school game that used to draw 2,000.

The popularity of the top-level Division I programs also has hurt attendance at the smaller Division I programs and on down through Division II and III. At Kentucky, only a handful of our games aren't televised because of conference restrictions, and there's no question that has damaged attendance at Eastern, Murray, Morehead and our state's smaller colleges and universities. There are four elements to having a good game: quality players, excellent coaches, competent officials and people in the stands. When you have near-empty arenas, it affects the quality of play. No question about it. So we have to ask ourselves, "When is enough enough?" More is not necessarily better. Yet, when you're the athletics director at a place like Kentucky, you can hardly say no to TV exposure. You need the money to meet your budget and your conference obligations.

So we're right back to the concept of the double-edged sword. On the one hand, universities, conferences and the NCAA are paid a fortune for the right to televise our games. But on the other, we have to surrender some of our control to TV. When you go for the big bucks, you've got to give TV a 9 o'clock starting time every now and then. Obviously, that's not in the best interest of the student-athlete. So the question ultimately comes, how much control are you willing to give up? In the NCAA's new contract with CBS, there's no starting time later than 9:30 p.m. in any time zone. That's not great, but it's the best we can do. And we must admit that TV has really helped the NCAA stimulate fan interest by helping us develop a national tournament. If our team is sent to the West Regional, for example, a lot of our fans can't afford to go there, but at least they can see it on TV.

One thing I want to make clear, however, is that CBS absolutely, positively has no impact on the NCAA Tournament's at-large selections, its seedings or its pairings. I know a lot of fans don't believe that. They think that Billy

Packer is virtually a de facto member of the committee. I just wish everybody who believes that could sit in on the committee meetings.

Chapter 14
Inside the Tournament
Selection Committee

I t's rather fitting that for two decades the NCAA Division I Men's Basketball Committee held its annual selection meeting in Kansas City, near the home of Harry Truman. It was Truman who once said of being President, "If you can't stand the heat, get out of the kitchen." That's also true of being a member of the committee. No matter how hard the members try to be fair in every respect, there's always going to be criticism. Some teams are angry about being left out. Others are upset about where they have to play or who they have to play against or where they're seeded. It's a thankless job, in that respect, but also one of the most exciting and challenging responsibilities that you can have as a college sports administrator.

I was on the committee briefly when I was in the SEC office as an associate commissioner. In fact, I went to the 1981 Final Four in Philadelphia to kind of get broken in. When I took the Vanderbilt job and got back into coaching, I got an interesting call from Tom Jernstedt, an NCAA assistant commissioner who had much to do with running the tournament.

"We're going to have to make a change," Tom said.

"Where does it say that you can't be a coach and be on the committee?" I shot back.

After a moment, Tom realized I was joking. No coach had been on the committee since Ohio State's Fred Taylor back in the 1960s. To have a coach on the committee would absolutely be the worst possible thing for both the coach and the committee.

In the early 1990s, when veteran Dayton Athletics Director Tom Frericks died, I was asked to fill out Tom's last year on the committee. After that, I was asked to remain a member. I eventually reached the point where I was named to serve a two-year term as chairman, covering the 1997-98 and 1998-99 seasons. Needless to say, I was thrilled and honored. Of all the committees I've served on, the two most significant are the tournament committee and the rules committee. The rules committee goes right to the guts of the game, and I'm proud to have been part of the group that brought in positive changes such as the three-point shot, the shot clock and the coaches box.

The tournament committee consists of nine athletics directors or administrators, and the glue that holds it together is the staff that the NCAA assigns to the committee. People such as Tom Jernstedt, Dave Cawood and many others have provided invaluable help over the years. The staff works on the tournament on a year-round basis, dealing with everything from preparing game sites to dealing with the coaches (through the National Association of Basketball Coaches) and the media (through the U.S. Basketball Writers Association). For these dedicated staff people, it's a full time labor of love. So the staff is the glue and the committee is the policy-maker.

If you'll go down the list of the committee's members over the years, you'll see the names of many of the NCAA's most important leaders. I'm talking about people such as Bernie Shively, Arnie Ferrin, Dick Shrider, Ben Carnevale, Dave Gavitt, Vic Bubas, Tom Butters, Dick Schultz, Cedric Dempsey and so many more. These were the folks who painstakingly shaped the philosophies that exist today. They were the visionaries who guided the tournament's growth to the point where it's now, in my opinion, the major sporting event of the year. A lot of sports have one-day events such as the Kentucky Derby or the Super Bowl, but this is a national championship that runs over three weeks. One really good thing we've done in recent years is have a working meeting between the current committee and committee alumni. It is remarkable how involved the alumni get. The current committee gets to pick their brains, and the alumni get to say things like, "You've got too much TV," or, "Why the late starting times?" It's really been a big help to the committee to tap into that kind of expertise.

For those of us who remember the days when the tournament was mainly a regional thing and didn't even have a national TV deal for the Final Four, the growth has been staggering. In the late 1950s and throughout the '60s, Freedom Hall in Louisville was host to the Final Four six times and Memorial Coliseum in Lexington was the site of several regionals. It was a financial issue more than anything. Where else were you going to have it? Freedom Hall was the biggest arena in the country and the largest on-campus venue was in Lexington.

In those days, the brackets were pretty well established along geographical lines. If you were a Kentucky fan, for example, you knew that the Southeastern Conference champion always was assigned to the Mideast Regional. So you could make your travel and hotel arrangements in October, if you wished. Even during that great run UCLA had from 1964 through '75, winning 10 national titles in 12 years, all they essentially had to do to get into the West Regional was beat Southern Cal. They never had to play anybody outside their region until the Final Four.

But as the tournament grew until it reached its current size of 64 teams (30 conference champions, 34 at-large selections for the 1999 event), the committee determined that it would be a true national championship. That became the committee's basic mission statement. In other words, there were no guarantees. Any team could be sent any-where. Geographical considerations meant little or nothing. Everything would be based on seedings, even if it meant sending North Carolina to Phoenix or UCLA to Orlando.

The committee also decided years ago that as many peo-ple as possible should be allowed to see the Final Four. So, essentially, that ruled out holding it in traditional basketball arenas such as Freedom Hall and going almost exclusively to domed stadiums. Basketball purists such as myself didn't nec-essarily like that, but there was no other choice. How are you going to deny the Final Four experience to 20,000 people? As it has turned out, even the fans who don't have a great seat seem willing to accept that just to be a part of it. For its part, the committee has tried to make the domes as basketball-friendly, and fan-friendly, as possible. I think we achieved that at San Antonio, St. Petersburg and Indianapolis.

The other thing about site selection, especially at the regional and subregional levels, is that you try to spread the tournament to the best sites available in geographical areas. Unless you go to domes, there aren't that many good sites for regionals. The committee tends to look for places that have proven they can put on a good show for the teams and the fans. Things such as transportation, hotels and restaurants must be considered. When you've got eight teams coming in for a subregional, for example, trans-portation becomes an important issue. You want to spread the tournament around as much as possible, keeping some geographical balance, but you've got to pick places that can handle all the demands. In recent years, it has become a rule of thumb to make the following year's Final Four site a regional host so that you can have a sort of dry run.

Let me try to explain what it's like to be a committee member in a typical year.

After the Final Four is completed, the committee immediately turns its attention to the next year — and beyond. In May, the committee meets with the NABC to find out what the coaches want. This is a very important meeting. Maybe CBS, which has been our broadcast partner since the early 1980s, has asked for additional interviews. We have to ask the coaches, "Where do you guys stand on this?" There was a time, years ago, when the NABC had a suspicion about the so-called "non-basketball guys" on the committee. For example, Roy Kramer of Vanderbilt and Tom Butters of Duke didn't have basketball backgrounds. So you would hear, "What do Kramer and Butters know?" One year Jud Heathcote of Michigan State came before the committee and really let us have it. But in the last few years, we've been able to help the NABC board understand how and why the committee is selected. Some of the best contributors have been the "non-basketball guys" because they bring fresh insights to the table.

At some point we also meet with the U.S. Basketball

Writers to discuss their concerns about credentials and seating, that sort of thing. As the tournament has grown in popularity, more media people want to cover it. However, even in domed stadiums, we can accommodate only so many requests. So the staff developed a credentialing formula based, for example, on circulation in the case of newspapers. We also have been re-evaluating the number of courtside seats that go to the writers. We think that creates a "dead" seating area that doesn't translate well on TV and that denies prime seating to fans. Naturally, the writers don't want to give up their seats on the grounds that they need to be close to the action to produce the best and most accurate stories possible. This promises to be a long-running battle.

In December, the committee meets to begin planning for what's become known as "March Madness." One reason for having members from every geographical region is that every team probably will be seen by someone on the committee at one time or another. As a former coach, I can tell you there's no substitute for seeing a team in person. All the ratings and computer stuff are just guides. So the committee members are urged to familiarize themselves, either in person or on TV, with as many teams around the country as possible, but particularly those in their areas. As the season unfolds, the committee members frequently talk on the phone, comparing notes.

When the committee arrives the weekend of the conference tournaments in early March, every member wants to be armed as fully as possible to do the job. I get the feeling that sometimes the public thinks we're a bunch of 1930s-style power brokers, wearing green visors and meeting in a smoke-filled room. But that's just not the case. Instead of chomping on cigars, we eat a lot of ice cream and brownies. I remember McKinley Boston of Minnesota, one of the so-called "non-basketball guys" who served on the committee, characterizing the committee's meeting as a "10-pound weekend." He was right on the money. When you're cooped up that long it's hard not to gain a few pounds.

We meet in a hotel suite. In our main meeting room there's a huge board where the brackets and seedings are posted. Nobody is allowed to touch it except the staff member in charge of it. If committee members were allowed to begin moving teams around on the board, that would lead to chaos. In another room, we have a bank of TV sets so we can keep up with what's going on in the conference tournaments. We need to be ready to react if a heavy favorite gets upset early, or if a darkhorse team gets hot and wins its conference tournament, as was the case with N.C. State and Georgia in 1983.

One of the first things we do is to ask every member to list 30 teams, not including his (or her) school, that should be in the tournament. Anybody that gets named on all nine ballots is automatically in. Generally, this will be somewhere between four and 12 teams. The real no-brainers.

As the weekend progresses, you sort through this thing and it changes constantly. The staff sees to it that we have immediate access to up-to-date RPI ratings and other information. When you get down to those last eight or 10 teams, they all start looking alike. I remember Tom Butters always cautioned us about giving every team our full consideration. "You can always play your way out of a bad seed," he would say, "so let's be sure we get the right teams in." At the end, you have to go with the best judgments of nine people. When you get to the bottom teams you assign three to each member and ask them to completely research those teams and their statistics. Then they make their cases — and there are times when people feel strongly about a team — and then we vote. All votes are secret ballots. In my case, I would always put on my coaching hat and ask myself, "Okay, if I were coaching and had my choice of playing X, Y or Z, which one would I most not want to play?"

Once the teams are selected your real work begins. If you don't seed properly, you can't get balanced brackets. All 64 teams are given a numerical rank in the seeding process. Then you just really pick the teams apart, ever mindful of all the rules and restrictions that have been adopted over the years. For example, no team can play on its home floor. Teams from the same conference can't meet until a regional final. Each of the first three teams selected from a conference should be placed in different regions. And so forth and so on. This part of it can get very tedious.

You start by identifying the top four seeds in the country, which isn't as easy as you might think. Then you pick the next four. When you get into the middle of the bracket, picking the four No. 8 seeds and the four No. 9 seeds, it can get very difficult. Even when we get down to the No. 12 through No. 16 seeds, we try to be very careful. One year we looked at who Coppin State had played out of its league and moved it up over somebody with a better record. That's where the strength of schedule kicks in. We don't always go strictly by the computer information.

On what has become known as "Selection Sunday," the day of reckoning, the national TV show at 6 p.m., EST, adds to the pressure. After the brackets have been set, the chairman gives the CBS people a briefing about the bracket. That's the first thing they get and they've had absolutely no input into our decisions. Usually that happens around 4 p.m., but the committee has been known to push the deadline as late as 4:45. Then the committee has to prep the chair so he doesn't go on national TV and make a damn fool of himself. The last thing the committee does before it leaves the room is put the 64 teams in a traditional bracket and take a last look at it. Sometimes, looking at the board, you're actually surprised to see who's playing who because you've been so focused on the seeding process.

During the TV show, the chair has to explain why this team got in and that one didn't. Why this team has to travel far and that one doesn't. Then you meet with the print media to go over the same stuff. By this time, the staff is working with our TV partners to review game times. You don't want a situation, for example, where North Carolina and N.C. State are playing at the same time. You don't want to force the local stations into having to make a choice as to which game they'll carry. The game times are announced on Monday.

One of the committee's final responsibilities is the assignment of game officials. We pick 96 officials out of a pool submitted to us by Hank Nichols, who's in charge of officiating for the NCAA. Then we work with Hank to assign those 96 officials to specific games. Some coaches think that committee members can influence which officials are assigned to which games. But that's not true. In every situation, there are checks and balances.

I would describe that weekend as the ultimate male-bonding experience, except that we now have our first female on the committee. I've never left one of those meetings feeling completely satisfied. But I've also never left thinking that the whole process was anything except nine people doing their level best to be fair. When I look at the tournament committee and the pressure that everyone is under, I see remarkably few instances where tempers

279

flared or mistakes were made.

After the field is selected, seeded and bracketed, the committee members don't get much time to rest. We have a committee member and an NCAA staff member at every tournament site. At every site we want everything as close to the same as we can possibly make it. It's up to the committee member to make sure that the sportsmanship code is enforced in regard to bench decorum, baiting officials, things like that.

When I was first on the committee, they assigned me to a subregional held at Cincinnati's Riverfront Coliseum, which hadn't been used for basketball in quite awhile. They had to brush dust off the rims and backboards. The NCAA sent Dave Cawood along to marshall me through this thing. My first big test came when Randy Ayers, then the coach at Ohio State, became completely frustrated with the officials even though he had a big lead. He was on the brink of getting out of hand when I went up to him and said, "Calm down, Randy … You don't want to be the first coach in NCAA Tournament history to get a technical foul with a 30-point lead."

In 1995, during a subregional in Boise, Idaho, there was an incident involving Bob Knight, my old friend, and a press-conference moderator. It boiled down to a miscommunication about whether Bob was going to appear at the press conference, but Bob made matters worse by cursing the moderator in front of the media. Eventually, the committee fined Bob $30,000. I was the only one who didn't want to fine him that amount. Instead, I wanted to suspend him from his next NCAA Tournament game. I'm not sure fines mean anything. But the one thing that coaches and players don't want to give up is the privilege of participating. Bob and I got cross-ways over that. But I believed he was wrong.

One good thing we've done in recent years is take the committee and form subcommittees to deal with ticketing and site selection, the basketball writers, the coaches, the officials and our partners at CBS. These subcommittees function throughout the year, but they really zero in at Final Four time. In the future, I'd like to see the committee get away from late starting times, demand continual refinement of the statistical data and, most importantly, continue to work very hard to foster strong relationships with its TV partner, the coaches, the writers and the local organizing committees at each tournament site.

When I chaired the TV subcommittee, I felt we were able to move from a business relationship to more of a partnership. We had some tough, straight-up talks with CBS at the subcommittee level. We gave CBS some of the things it wanted, but we protected some other things. It's easy to get frustrated and say, "Oh, hell no, we're not doing anymore for TV." But you really can't do that. It always must be remembered that most of the people who see the tournament see it through the eyes of TV.

But that certainly doesn't mean you let them put microphones in the huddle. And it will never mean that TV will get any input into selection, seeding and brackets. The integrity of the committee is the key to the whole thing. You can't imagine how difficult it is to be an athletics director on the committee and have a high-profile coach on your campus. If your team isn't selected, you know what you're going to face when you get home. But you just have to pick it up and keep going. I can remember leaving for the meeting one year and having Rick Pitino say, "Just don't send us out West." Well, naturally, that's exactly where the committee sent us.

Chapter 15
The Last Hurrah

I didn't decide to retire for family health reasons. Although I had a pacemaker implanted in October 1999, to correct an irregular heartbeat, and although Evelyn continues her battle with leukemia, we're doing rather well for a couple of senior citizens who have been married for 48 years. I just think it's time, that's all. After more than 50 years in intercollegiate athletics, I'm ready to move on. I want to maintain an active role, perhaps as a consultant, but it will be at my own pace for a change. Somebody once told me that "No" is a complete sentence, and I'm starting to say "No" more often, which has never been my nature.

Whenever I'm asked about my legacy, I don't know what to say. If there is such a thing, it's up to others to decide, not me. I just hope that if and when I'm remembered, it will be as somebody who tried to make a difference as both a coach and an administrator. By that, I mean trying to be a mentor as well as a coach. Caring about student-athletes as human beings instead of just looking at them as a labor force whose main task is to win games and make money. Pushing them to get an education and teaching them how to live and be productive citizens, no matter whether they're going to be NBA players or insurance agents or farmers. If we are to maintain our integrity as educators, that always must be at the core of our philosophy.

But when I talk about making a difference, I don't mean that it always has to be on a grand scale. It can be on a small scale that will never get you any recognition from the media. You just do it because you can and because it's right. When I was in St. Petersburg, Russia, for the 1994 Goodwill Games, I met a young girl named Anna Karabanova. She was one of the interpreters, and I was impressed with her work ethic and how bright she was. But her future looked bleak. This was just after the breakup of the Soviet Union, when those people were really struggling.

When I learned that her dream was to study in the United States, I thought, "I can't help the Russian people, but maybe I can help this girl." I never met her parents, but they put her on a plane and sent her to me when she was 16 years old. You talk about a leap of faith. For all they knew, I could have been Jack the Ripper. But she became a student at the University of Kentucky and thrived. Evelyn and I helped her some financially and she worked in the athletics department for a while. She had a double major in language and political science, and in May 1999, she graduated with honors. Now she's trying to decide whether to go to graduate school or return to Russia to be with her father. (Her mother died while she was in high school.) But she's just a wonderful person and I look forward to seeing what she does with the rest of her life.

Did she take a risk in leaving her home to come here? You bet. But she's also a perfect example of my belief in the importance of risking failure to achieve success. I'm talking about a calculated risk, not something wild that has no chance to succeed. As a coach, you never want a player who's not willing to take a risk. There are some players who can have a perfect line in the boxscore — no missed shots, no turnovers, no fouls. But that's not necessarily a perfect game. You'll never win with players who always want to do the safe thing and aren't willing to risk making a mistake.

When I talk about the risks in my career, maybe some of them are illusionary. Maybe it wasn't such a big risk to come to UK as a player, to take the Transylvania job before I was ready, to try to integrate the program at Alabama at a difficult time in American history, to go back to coaching at age 50 after a year on the sidelines and to take the athletics director's job at Kentucky in the midst of a crisis. Maybe it wasn't that big of a risk to hire a Division II football coach or an African-American basketball coach. At the same time, none of those moves was a guaranteed success. I just felt strongly, in each case, that my chances of success were better than 50-50.

Now, at the risk of sounding sanctimonious, I would like to emphasize a few points that I've addressed earlier.

First, we must — must! — continue to educate young people about the problems inherent in drugs, alcohol and gambling. I'll never forget hearing about the Jason Watts tragedy. It was the morning of Sunday, Nov. 15, 1998. The previous day, our football team defeated Vanderbilt, 55-17, to assure us of our first seven-win season since 1984 and a bowl invitation. But all my good feelings about that disappeared when I heard that there had been a car accident near Somerset in which Jason had been seriously injured and a couple of students killed. When I learned later that all three were legally drunk, it triggered all the emotions and fears that I've had about alcohol since my childhood.

I remembered the times I saw Dad trying to drive after having too much to drink. My daughter, Deborah, totaled a car when we lived in Tuscaloosa and then did it again when we were in Nashville. When she got charged with a DUI after the Nashville accident, she wanted help and chose the 30-day program at the Cumberland Heights treatment center. It was a life-changing experience that affected the whole family. When it's your own daughter and you see the pain and suffering — but also the courage — it has a profound effect on you. But Deb achieved sobriety and she has maintained it. I'm so proud of her. As a result of her experiences, Evelyn and I both got involved in Alanon and worked through a whole lot of issues, many of them related to my dad, that had been sitting there for years.

As a coach, an administrator and a parent, the thing that kept running through my mind was, "When are you helping people and when are you enabling them?" There's such an awareness on a personal level. As a coach or administrator, you ask yourself, "What more could I have done that might have made a difference?" When the facts of the Jason Watts incident became clear, my reaction was, "Dammit, enough is enough!" This is something that had been brewing here (no pun intended) for quite a while. Despite all of our educational and monitoring efforts, alcohol abuse was becoming a real problem. So that really triggered the thought that we were going to a zero-tolerance approach about the whole issue. The message to our student-athletes was that if they were going to drink, they were going to do it responsibly or risk losing their scholarships. And if they were doing it while under age, they were violating the law. It's a policy that will require constant tweaking and monitoring, but I'm encouraged with the early results.

As I've said earlier, I feel just as strongly about the evils of gambling. One of my worst fears is that we're on the brink of another point-shaving scandal that would have a devastating effect on college basketball at a time when the sport is more popular than ever. If the media won't stop printing the Las Vegas gambling line, I would hope they would at least be responsible enough to join in the effort to educate young people about how sports gambling can ruin their lives. I would also like to respectfully encourage the media to give more publicity to student-athletes who succeed academically. As it is, it almost seems as if you only hear about the one who flunks out.

Second, I would encourage universities to keep the proper balance between athletics and academics. Athletics is only a service arm of a university, sort of like agricultural extension agents out in the state. But if you're not careful, the tail can start wagging the dog. So we need to put into perspective the whole business about an athletics department's relationship to its university. It's important, but it's not why the university exists. Even some university presidents don't understand that while athletics has become a big business, it's only a drop in the bucket when you consider the university's billion-dollar budget.

But the financial issue is going to be with us for awhile. Going back to when UK and other universities decided to force their athletics departments to be financially self-sufficient, that created a kind of business mindset that causes conflict. When you look at the gate receipts, the radio-TV revenues and the corporate spon-sorships, it's easy to make the case that the athletes should be paid some kind of stipend. It's a delicate issue — the old double-edged sword again. With 400 athletes on scholarship at UK, that's a lot of expense for the uni-versity in room, board, tuition and fees. A four-year scholarship at a Division I university can be worth as much as $125,000. Is that adequate compensation for a student-athlete? I think so.

Third, looking at the future of the NCAA, I think gover-nance is going to be a big issue. The new NCAA structure eliminated the one-vote, one-school concept to a more rep-resentative concept. The power conferences don't have a lot in common with the lesser ones. They want more freedom to make their own rules and get a larger share of the prof-its. With the Bowl Championship Series system in football, the power conferences have banded together. There's some thought to doing the same thing in basketball. That power struggle is going to continue for the foreseeable future.

In retrospect, when I think about what I wanted to do when I came back to UK, I feel good about where we are as I prepare to retire. There always will be things that you could have done different or better, but overall I feel really good. We've kept the student-athlete at the heart of our program. We strive for total compliance with the rules of the university, the SEC and the NCAA. We're nationally competitive in a broad-based sports program. We exude recognizable class. (As a U.S. Supreme Court justice once said about pornography, "I'm not sure I can define it, but I can recognize it every time.") We've practiced good fiscal responsibility. And in the area of sports medicine, I think we've done things for the benefit of the student-athlete that will have a lasting effect.

So I feel good about where we're leaving the thing, and I'm looking forward to the rest of my life. On a professional level, my agreement with the university is that I will be available for consulting for four years. If they need me, I'll be there. I also may do some consulting with the NCAA on a volunteer basis and I intend to stay active on the FIBA Central Board. But what I really want to do is spend a lot of quality time with Evelyn, my three children and my five grandchildren. A lot of the time I wasn't there for my children, especially during the Alabama years. I was just gone a lot, trying to build a team and integrate the program. I tried to make that up by emphasizing quality of time over quantity of time. And Evelyn always was great about not letting me bring basketball home with me. When I was home, that was family time.

We're going to stay in Lexington, though, because of her leukemia, we're also going to spend a lot of time at Treasure Cay, Abaco, in the Bahamas. The wintertime climate there will be much better for her. But I also want the flexibility to visit old friends. There are a lot of people from different stops in my career that I haven't had the opportunity to spend time with in recent years. I'd like to get up to Boston, for example, to visit Rick and Joanne Pitino, along with Dave and Julie Gavitt. Who knows what else? Bonefishing always has been one of my passions. I would like to learn to paint. I'm not interested in doing more writing, although maybe I'll finish my doctorate.

I just can't say enough about Evelyn. She and I were friends before we fell in love. Her exposure to competitive athletics helped her understand me and enabled me to bounce problems off her. At the same time, we've also been able to give each other the space to do our own thing. We don't crowd each other. She's the most caring person I've ever known, and that comes through in everything she has done — child-rearing, grand-parenting, volunteer work, whatever. I've watched her grow as a person, and that has given me as much joy as anything I've done in my career. When she was diagnosed with lymphoma, it occurred to me for the first time that she might die before me. That changed the way I looked at life. So we're just going to take it slow, get away with each other, and go from there.

In closing, I would just like to say that I feel like Lou Gehrig. At his retirement from the New York Yankees, he said he felt like "the luckiest man on the face of the earth." My career didn't exactly turn out the way I dreamed as a youngster in Fort Lauderdale, when all I wanted to do was be a Major League Baseball star. But it has been a wonderful, exciting, challenging ride. I've been blessed with incredible coaches, mentors, teammates, players, bosses, friends and, most importantly, family members.

Fortunately, my calculated risks worked out for me. And if I've made a small difference in a few people's lives, well, that will give this gray-haired grandpa something happy to think about when I'm out there in the shallow waters on a warm summer's day, waiting for some doggoned bonefish to come along and make a fool out of me.

For the record

Transylvania

1951-52	5-15
1952-53	6-12
1955-56	9-9
1956-57	16-10
1957-58	18-12
1958-59	15-10
1959-60	19-7
1960-61	16-12
1961-62	15-13
1962-63	20-9
1963-64	7-17
1965-66	6-17
1966-67	14-10
1967-68	14-12

Alabama

1968-69	4-20
1969-70	8-18
1970-71	10-16
1971-72	18-8
1972-73	22-8
1973-74	22-4
1974-75	22-5
1975-76	23-5
1976-77	25-6
1977-78	17-10
1978-79	22-11
1979-80	18-12

Vanderbilt

1981-82	15-13
1982-83	19-14
1983-84	14-15
1984-85	11-17
1985-86	13-15
1986-87	18-16
1987-88	20-11
1988-89	19-14

Family: Wife Evelyn; children Deborah, Tracy and Martin; and five grandchildren, Katie, Madison, Zach, Joshua and Sheridan.

Date of Birth: February 2, 1930.

Education: Kentucky, 1952 (Bachelor's); Kentucky, 1957 (Master's).

College Athletic Career: Letterman on Kentucky's 1951 national championship basketball team; pitched for UK baseball team.

Professional Athletic Career: Pitcher in New York Yankees minor league system.

Professional Positions: Head basketball coach, Transylvania University, 1952-53, 1956-64, 1966-68; Head basketball coach, University of Alabama, 1969-80; Assistant Commissioner, Southeastern Conference, 1980-81; Head basketball coach, Vanderbilt University, 1982-89; Director of Athletics, University of Kentucky, 1989-2000.

Coaching Achievements: Associated Press Southeastern Conference Coach of the Year 1972, '76, '88, '89; United Press International SEC Coach of the Year 1972, '78, '88; U.S. Olympic Team Assistant, 1984.

Professional Achievements: Member of Board of Directors, National Association of Basketball Coaches (NABC), 1977-80, 1981-89; Chairman of NCAA Basketball Rules Committee, 1979-85; Vice President, USA Basketball, 1988-92; President, USA Basketball, 1992-96; Chairman USA Basketball Games Committee, 1988-92; Member of NCAA Division I Basketball Committee, 1992-99; Chairman, NCAA Division I Basketball Committee, 1998-99; Chairman, NCAA Basketball Officiating Committee, 1992-95; Member, Federation of International Basketball Associations (FIBA) Central Board, 1994-2000; Given John Bunn Award by Naismith Basketball Hall of Fame, recognizing lifetime of contribution to basketball; Given Naismith Award by the Atlanta Tipoff Club in recognition of service to basketball, 1999.